THE CRIME OF IMPRISONMENT

THE CRIME OF IMPRISONMENT

by George Bernard Shaw

Illustrated by
WILLIAM GROPPER

GREENWOOD PRESS, PUBLISHERS
NEW YORK

TABLE OF CONTENTS

A WORD FROM THE PUBLISHERS

The publishers of the Philosophical Library deem it a privilege to be able to present, in book form, the now famous treatise on IMPRISONMENT, by George Bernard Shaw. This treatise originally constituted a preface to the report of Lord Olivier on English and American prison conditions, during the period immediately following the last war. The investigation, as well as the report and Mr. Shaw's treatise, were prepared in behalf of the British Labor Research Office in an effort to revise the common system of imprisonment.

The publishers feel that society should benefit greatly by Mr. Shaw's penetrating discussion, the present post-war period being so similar in its nature to the one following World War I.

FOREWORD

When I was a boy in my teens in Dublin I was asked by an acquaintance of mine who was clerk to a Crown Solicitor, and had business in prisons, whether I would like to go through Mountjoy Prison, much as he might have asked me whether I would like to go through the Mint, or the cellars at the docks. I accepted the invitation. What struck me most was that the place was as bright and clean as whitewash and scrubbing and polish could make it, with all the warders looking thoroughly respectable, and all the prisoners ruffianly and degenerate, except one tall delicate figure tramping round in the exercise ring, a Lifer by the color of his cap, who had chopped up his family with a hatchet, and been recommended to mercy on account of his youth. I thought, and still think, imprisonment for life a curious sort of mercy. My main impression of the others, and the one that has stuck longest and hardest, was that as it was evidently impossible to reform such men, it was useless to torture them, and dangerous to release them.

I have never been imprisoned myself; but in my first years as a public speaker I had to volunteer for prison martyrdom in two Free Speech conflicts with the police. As my luck would have it, on the first occasion the police capitulated on the eve of the day on which I had undertaken to address a prohibited meeting and refuse to pay a fine; and on the second a rival political organization put up a rival martyr, and, on a division, carried his election over my head, to my great relief. These incidents are not very impressive now; but the fact that my acquaintance with the subject of the following essay began with the sight of an actual prison, and that twice afterwards I was for a week or so firmly convinced that I was about to spend at least a fortnight and possibly a month in the cells, gave me an interest in the subject less perfunctory that that of the ordinary citizen to whom prison is only a reference in the police news, denoting simply a place where dishonest and violent people are very properly locked up.

This comfortable ignorance, by the way, is quite commonly shared by judges. A Lord Chief Justice of England, grieved at hearing from a lady of social importance that her son had been sent to prison as a Conscientious Objector, told her that he hoped she would get to see him often, and keep up his spirits with frequent letters, and send him in nice things to eat. He was amazed to learn from her that he might just as well have suggested a motor ride every afternoon and a visit to the opera in the evening. He had been sentencing people all through his judicial career to terms of imprisonment, some of them for life, without knowing that it meant anything more than being confined to the house and wearing a dress with broad arrows all over it. No doubt he thought, quite rightly, that such confinement was bad enough for anybody, however wicked.

I had no such illusions about prison life. My political activities often brought me into contact with men of high character and ability who had been victims of modern forms of persecution under the very elastic heading of treason, sedition, obstruction, blasphemy, offences against press laws, and so forth. I knew that Karl Marx had declared that British prisons were the cruelest in the world; and I thought it quite probable that he was right. I knew Prince Peter Kropotkin, who, after personal experience of the most villainous convict prisons in Siberia and the best model prison in France, said that they were both so bad that the difference was not worth talking about. What with European "politicals" and amnestied Irish Fenians, those who, like myself, were in the way of meeting such people could hardly feel easy in their consciences about the established methods of handling criminals.

Also I was in occasional touch with certain efforts made by the now extinct Humanitarian League, and by a little Society called the Police and Public Vigilance Society, to call attention to the grievances of prisoners. The League dealt with punishments; the Society, which was really an agitation conducted by one devoted man with very slender means, the late James Timewell, tried to obtain redress for people who alleged that they had been the victims of petty frame-ups by the police. But the witnesses on whose testimony these two bodies had to proceed were mostly either helpless creatures who could not tell the truth or scoundrels who would not tell it. The helpless creatures told you what they wanted to believe themselves: the scoundrels told you what they wanted you to believe.

Anyone who has tried to find out what war is like from our demobilized soldiers will understand. Their consciousness is limited and utterly uncritical; their memory is inaccurate and confused; their judgment is perverted by personal dislikes and vanities; and as to reflection, reason, self-criticism, and the rest of the intellectual counterchecks, they have no more of them than a mouse has of mathematics. If this is the case with normal men like soldiers, even less is to be expected from subnormal men like criminals. Neither the Humanitarian League nor Mr. Timewell could rouse general public compunction with such testimony, or attract special subscriptions enough to enable them to conduct a serious investigation. And John Galsworthy had not then arisen to smite our conscience with such plays as The Silver Box and Justice.

This situation was changed by the agitation
for Votes for Women and the subsequent war of
1914-18, both of which threw into prison an un-
precedented number of educated, critical, public
spirited, conscientious men and women who under
ordinary circumstances would have learnt no
more about prisons than larks learn about coal
mines. They came out of prison unembittered by
their personal sufferings: their grievance was
the public grievance of the whole prison system
and its intense irreligiousness. In prison they
had been capable of observing critically what
they saw; and out of prison they were able to
describe it. The official whitewash of the Prison
Commissioners could not impose on them. They
and their friends had money enough to take an
office and engage a secretarial staff, besides sup-
plying some voluntary educated labor. They
formed a committee with Lord Olivier as chair-
man, which investigated the condition of English
prisons and incidentally read some interesting
reports of American ones. Eventually they issued
their report as a volume entitled English Prisons
Today, edited by Stephen Hobhouse and Fenner
Brockway, who had both been in prison during
the war.

I was a member of that committee; and the
essay which follows was written as a preface to
the report. But I did not find it possible to keep
a thorough sifting of the subject within the lim-

its of the sixth commandment, on which Mr. Hobhouse took an uncompromising stand. Fortunately my friends Sidney and Beatrice Webb were just then reinforcing the work of the committee by issuing the volume of their monumental history of English Local Government which deals with prisons. By transferring my preface to their book I was able to secure the intended publicity for it, and to please everybody concerned, myself included.

I give this history of the essay lest it should be taken as a fanciful exercise by a literary man making up the subject out of his own head. I have not made a parade of facts and figures because my business is to change the vindictive attitude towards criminals which has made the facts possible; but I know the facts better, apparently, than the Prison Commissioners, and relevant figures quite as well.

G.B.S.

THE SPIRIT IN WHICH TO READ
THIS ESSAY

Imprisonment as it exists today is a worse crime than any of those committed by its victims; for no single criminal can be as powerful for evil, or as unrestrained in its exercise, as an organized nation. Therefore, if any person is addressing himself to the perusal of this dreadful subject in the spirit of a philanthropist bent on reforming a necessary and beneficent public institution, I beg him to put it down and go about some other business. It is just such reformers who have in the past made the neglect, oppression, corruption, and physical torture of the old common gaol the pretext for transforming it into that diabolical den of torment, mischief, and damnation, the modern model prison.

If, on the contrary, the reader comes as a repentant sinner, let him read on.

The difficulty in finding repentant sinners when this crime is in question has two roots. The first is that we are all brought up to believe that we may inflict injuries on anyone against whom we can make out a case of moral inferiority. We have this thrashed into us in our childhood by the infliction on ourselves of such injuries by our

[13]

parents and teachers, or indeed by any elder who happens to be in charge of us. The second is that we are all now brought up to believe, not that the king can do no wrong, because kings have been unable to keep up that pretence, but that Society can do no wrong. Now not only does Society commit more frightful crimes than any individual, king or commoner: it legalizes its crimes, and forges certificates of righteousness for them, besides torturing anyone who dares expose their true character. A society like ours, which will, without remorse, ruin a boy body and soul for life for trying to sell newspapers in a railway station, is not likely to be very tender to people who venture to tell it that its laws would shock the Prince of Darkness himself if he had not been taught from his earliest childhood to respect as well as fear them.

Consequently we have a desperately sophisticated public, as well as a quite frankly vindictive one. Judges spend their lives consigning their fellow-creatures to prison; and when some whisper reaches them that prisons are horribly cruel and destructive places, and that no creature fit to live should be sent there, they only remark calmly that prisons are not meant to be comfortable, which is no doubt the consideration that reconciled Pontius Pilate to the practice of crucifixion.

Society can do no wrong . . .

THE OBSTACLE OF STUPIDITY

Another difficulty is the sort of stupidity that comes from lack of imagination. When I tell people that I have seen with these eyes a man (no less a man than Richard Wagner, by the way) who once met a crowd going to see a soldier broken on the wheel by the crueller of the two legalized methods of carrying out that hideous sentence, they shudder, and are amazed to hear that what they call medieval torture was used in civilized Europe so recently. They forget that the punishment of half-hanging, unmentionably mutilating, beheading, and quartering, was on the British statute book within my own memory. The same people will read of a burglar being sentenced to ten years' penal servitude without turning a hair. They are like Ibsen's Peer Gynt, who was greatly reassured when he was told that the pains of hell are mental: he thought they cannot be so very bad if there is no actual burning brimstone. When such people are terrified by an outburst of robbery with violence, or Sadistically excited by reports of the White Slave traffic, they clamor to have sentences of two years' hard labor supplemented by a flogging, which is a joke by comparison. They will try to lynch a criminal who illtreats a child in some sensationally cruel

manner; but on the most trifling provocation they
will inflict on the child the prison demoralization
and the prison stigma which condemn it for the
rest of its life to crime as the only employment
open to a prison child. The public conscience
would be far more active if the punishment of imprisonment were abolished, and we went back to
the rack, the stake, the pillory, and the lash at
the cart's tail.

The objection to retrogression is not that such
punishments are more cruel than imprisonment.
They are less cruel, and far less permanently in-
jurious. The decisive objection to them is that
they are sports in disguise. The pleasure to the
spectators, and not the pain to the criminal, condemns them. People will go to see Titus Oates
flogged or Joan of Arc burnt with equal zest as
an entertainment. They will pay high prices for
a good view. They will reluctantly admit that
they must not torture one another as long as certain rules are observed; but they will hail a breach
of the rules with delight as an excuse for a bout
of cruelty. Yet they can be shamed at last into
recognizing that such exhibitions are degrading
and demoralizing; that the executioner is a wretch
whose hand no decent person cares to take; and
that the enjoyment of the spectators is fiendish.
We have then to find some form of torment which
can give no sensual satisfaction to the tormentor,

[17]

and which is hidden from public view. That is how imprisonment, being just such a torment, became the normal penalty. The fact that it may be worse for the criminal is not taken into account. The public is seeking its own salvation, not that of the lawbreaker. For him it would be far better to suffer in the public eye; for among the crowd of sightseers there might be a Victor Hugo or a Dickens, able and willing to make the sightseers think of what they are doing and ashamed of it. The prisoner has no such chance. He envies the unfortunate animals in the Zoo, watched daily by thousands of disinterested observers who never try to convert a tiger into a Quaker by solitary confinement, and would set up a resounding agitation in the papers if even the most ferocious maneater were made to suffer what the most docile convict suffers. Not only has the convict no such protection: the secrecy of his prison makes it hard to convince the public that he is suffering at all.

There is another reason for this incredulity. The vast majority of our city populations are inured to imprisonment from their childhood. The school is a prison. The office and the factory are prisons. The home is a prison. To the young who have the misfortune to be what is called well brought up it is sometimes a prison of inhuman severity. The children of John Howard, as far as their liberty was concerned, were treated very much as he insisted criminals should be treated, with the result that his children were morally disabled, like criminals. This imprisonment in the home, the school, the office, and the factory is kept up by browbeating, scolding, bullying, punishing, disbelief of the prisoner's statements and acceptance of those of the official, essentially as in a criminal prison. The freedom given by the adult's right to walk out of his prison is only a freedom to go into another or starve: he can choose the prison where he·is best treated: that is all. On the other hand, the imprisoned criminal is free from care as to his board, lodging, and clothing: he pays no taxes, and has no responsibilities. Nobody expects him to work as an unconvicted man must work if he is to keep his job: nobody expects him to do his work well, or cares twopence whether it is well done or not.

Under such circumstances it is very hard to convince the ordinary citizen that the criminal is not better off than he deserves to be, and indeed on the verge of being positively pampered. Judges, magistrates, and Home Secretaries are so commonly under the same delusion that people who have ascertained the truth about prisons have been driven to declare that the most urgent necessity of the situation is that every judge, magistrate. and Home Secretary should serve a six months' sentence incognito; so that when he is dealing out and enforcing sentences he should at least know what he is doing.

When we get down to the poorest and most oppressed of our population we find the conditions of their life so wretched that it would be impossible to conduct a prison humanely without making the lot of the criminal more eligible than that of many free citizens. If the prison does not underbid the slum in human misery, the slum will empty and the prison will fill. This does in fact take place to a small extent at present, because slum life at its worst is so atrocious that its victims, when they are intelligent enough to study alternatives instead of taking their lot blindly, conclude that prison is the most comfortable place to spend the winter in, and qualify themselves accordingly by committing an offence for which they will get six months. But this consideration affects only those people whose condition is not defended by any responsible publicist: the remedy is admittedly not to make the prison worse but the slum better. Unfortunately the admitted claims of the poor on life are pitifully modest. The moment the treatment of the criminal is decent and merciful enough to give him a chance of moral recovery, or, in incorrigible cases, to avoid making bad worse, the official descriptions of his lot become so rosy that a clamor arises against thieves and murderers being better off than honest and kindly men; for the official reports tell us only of the care that is taken of the prisoner and the advantages he enjoys, or can earn by good conduct, never of his sufferings; and the public is not imaginative or thoughtful enough to supply the deficiency.

What sane man, I ask the clamorers, would accept an offer of free board, lodging, clothing, waiters in attendance at a touch of the bell, medical treatment, spiritual advice, scientific ventilation and sanitation, technical instruction, liberal education, and the use of a carefully selected library, with regular exercise daily and sacred music at frequent intervals, even at the very best of the Ritz Hotels, if the conditions were that he should never leave the hotel, never speak, never sing, never laugh, never see a newspaper, and write only one sternly censored letter and have one miserable interview at long intervals through the bars of a cage under the eye of a warder? And when the prison is not the Ritz Hotel, when the lodging, the food, the bed, are all deliberately made so uncomfortable as to be instruments of torture, when the clothes are rags promiscuously worn by all your fellow-prisoners in turn with yourself, when the exercise is that of a turnspit, when the ventilation and sanitation are noisome, when the instruction is a sham, the education a fraud, when the doctor is a bully to whom your ailments are all malingerings, and the chaplain a moral snob with no time for anything but the distribution of unreadable books, when the waiters are bound by penalties not to speak to you except to give you an order or a rebuke, and then to address you as you would not dream of addressing your dog, when the manager holds over your head a continual threat of starvation and confinement in a punishment cell (as if your own cell were not punishment enough) then what man in his senses would voluntarily exchange even the most harassed freedom for such a life, much less wallow luxuriously in it, as the Punch burglar always does on paper the moment anyone suggests the slightest alleviation of the pains of imprisonment?

GIVING THEM HELL

Yet people cannot be brought to see this. They ask, first, what right the convict has to complain when he has brought it on himself by his own misconduct, and second, what he has to complain of. You reply that his grievances are silence, solitude, idleness, waste of time, and irresponsibility. The retort is, "Why call that torture, as if it were boiling oil or red hot irons or something like that? Why, I have taken a cottage in the country for the sake of silence and solitude; and I should be only too glad to get rid of my

responsibilities and waste my time in idleness like
a real gentleman. A jolly sight too well off, the
fellows are. I should give them hell."

Thus imprisonment is at once the most cruel
of punishments and the one that those who inflict
it without having ever experienced it cannot believe to be cruel. A country gentleman with a
big hunting stable will indignantly discharge a
groom and refuse him a reference for cruelly
thrashing a horse. But it never occurs to him
that his stables are horse prisons, and the stall a
cell in which it is quite unnatural for the horse
to be immured. In my youth I saw the great
Italian actress Ristori play Mary Stuart; and
nothing in her performance remains more vividly
with me than her representation of the relief of
Mary at finding herself in the open air after
months of imprisonment. When I first saw a stud
of hunters turned out to grass, they reminded me
so strongly of Ristori that I at once understood
that they had been prisoners in their stables, a
fact which, obvious as it was, I had not thought
of before. And this sort of thoughtlessness, being
continuous and unconscious, inflicts more suffering than all the malice and passion in the world.
In prison you get one piled on the other: to the
cruelty that is intended and contrived, that
grudges you even the inevitable relief of sleep,
and makes your nights miserable by plank beds
and the like, is added the worse cruelty that is

Giving them Hell 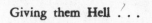...

not intended as cruelty, and, when its perpetrators can be made conscious of it at all, deludes them by a ghastly semblance of pampered indulgence.

And now comes a further complication. When people are at last compelled to think about what they are doing to our unfortunate convicts, they think so unsuccessfully and confusedly that they only make matters worse. Take for example the official list of the results aimed at by the Prison Commissioners. First, imprisonment must be "retributory" (the word vindictive is not in official use). Second, it must be deterrent. Third, it must be reformative.

Now, if you are to punish a man retributively, you must injure him. If you are to reform him, you must improve him. And men are not improved by injuries. To propose to punish and reform people by the same operation is exactly as if you were to take a man suffering from pneumonia, and attempt to combine punitive and curative treatment. Arguing that a man with pneumonia is a danger to the community, and that he need not catch it if he takes proper care of his health, you resolve that he shall have a severe lesson, both to punish him for his negligence and pulmonary weakness and to deter others from following his example. You therefore strip him naked, and in that condition stand him all night in the snow. But as you admit the duty of restoring him to health if possible, and discharging him with sound lungs, you engage a doctor to superintend the punishment and administer cough lozenges, made as unpleasant to the taste as possible so as not to pamper the culprit. A Board of Commissioners ordering such treatment would prove thereby that either they were imbeciles or else they were hotly in earnest about punishing the patient and not in the least in earnest about curing him.

When our Prison Commissioners pretend to combine punishment with moral reformation they are in the same dilemma. We are told that the reformation of the criminal is kept constantly in view; yet the destruction of the prisoner's self-respect by systematic humiliation is deliberately ordered and practised; and we learn from a chaplain that he "does not think it is good to give opportunity for the exercise of Christian and social virtues one towards another" among prisoners. The only consolation for such contradictions is their demonstration that, as the tormentors instinctively feel that they must be liars and hypocrites on the subject, their consciences cannot be very easy about the torment. But the contradictions are obvious here only because I put them on the same page. The Prison Commissioners keep them a few pages apart; and the average reader's memory, it seems, is not long enough to span the gap when his personal interests are not at stake.

Deterrence, which is the real object of the courts, has much more to be said for it, because it is neither simply and directly wicked like retribution, nor a false excuse for wickedness like reformation. It is an unquestionable fact that, by making rules and forcing those who break them to suffer so severely that others like them become afraid to break them, discipline can be maintained to a certain extent among creatures without sense enough to understand its necessity, or, if they do understand it, without conscience enough to refrain from violating it. This is the crude basis of all our disciplines: home discipline, school discipline, factory discipline, army and navy discipline, as well as of prison discipline, and of the whole fabric of criminal law. It is imposed not only by cruel rulers, but by unquestionably humane ones: the only difference being that the cruel rulers impose it with alacrity and gloat over its execution, and the humane rulers are driven to it reluctantly by the failure of their appeals to the consciences of people who have no conscience. Thus we find Mahomet, a conspicuously humane and conscientious Arab, keeping his fierce staff in order, not by unusual punishments, but by threats of a hell after death which he invented for the purpose in revolting detail of a kind which suggests that Mahomet had perhaps too much of the woman and the artist in him to know what would frighten a Bedouin most. Wellington, a general so humane that he sacrificed the exercise of a military genius of the first order to his moral horror of war and his freedom from its illusions, nevertheless hanged and flogged his soldiers mercilessly because he had learnt from experience that, as he put it, nothing is worse than impunity. All revolutions have been the work of men who, like Robespierre, were sentimental humanitarians and conscientious objectors to capital punishment and to the severities of military and prison discipline; yet all the revolutions have after a very brief practical experience been driven to Terrorism (the proper name of Deterrence) as ruthless as the Counter-Revolutionary Terror of Sulla, a late example being that of the Russian revolution of 1917. Whether it is Sulla, Robespierre, Trotsky, or the fighting mate of a sailing ship with a crew of loafers and wastrels, the result is the same: there are people to be dealt with who will not obey the law unless they are afraid to disobey it, and whose disobedience would mean disaster.

CRIME CANNOT BE KILLED
BY KINDNESS

It is useless for humanitarians to shirk this hard fact, and proclaim their conviction that all lawbreakers can be reformed by kindness. That may be true in many cases provided you can find a very gifted practitioner to take the worst ones in hand, with unlimited time and means to treat them. But if these conditions are not available, and a policeman and an executioner who will disable the wrongdoer instantaneously are available, the police remedy is the only practicable one, even for rulers filled with the spirit of the Sermon on the Mount. The late G. V. Foote, President of the English National Secular Society, a strenuous humanitarian, once had to persuade a very intimate friend of his, a much smaller and weaker man, to allow himself to be taken to an asylum for lunatics. It took four hours of humanitarian persuasion to get the patient from the first floor of his house to the cab door. Foote told me that he had not only recognized at once that no asylum attendant, with several patients to attend to, could possibly spend four hours in getting each of them downstairs, but found his temper so intolerably strained by the unnatural tax on his patience that if the breaking point had been reached, as it certainly would have been in the case of a warder or asylum attendant, he would have been far more violent, not to say savage, than if he had resorted to force at once, and finished the job in five minutes.

From resorting to this rational and practically compulsory use of kindly physical coercion to making it so painful that the victim will be afraid to give any trouble next time is a pretty certain step. In prisons the warders have to protect themselves against violence from prisoners, of which there is a constant risk and very well founded dread, as there are always ungovernably savage criminals who have little more power of refraining from furious assaults than some animals, including quite carefully bred dogs and horses, have of refraining from biting and savaging. The official punishment is flogging and putting in irons for months. But the immediate rescue of the assaulted warder has to be effected by the whole body of warders within reach; and whoever supposes that the prisoner suffers nothing more at their hands than the minimum of force necessary to restrain him knows nothing of prison life and less of human nature.

Any criticism of the deterrent theory of our prison system which ignores the existence of ungovernable savages will be discredited by the citation of actual cases. I should be passed over as a sentimentalist if I lost sight of them for the

moment. On any other subject I could dispose
of the matter by reminding my critics that hard
cases make bad law. On this subject I recognize
that the hard cases are of such a nature that
provision must be made for them. Indeed hard
cases may be said to be the whole subject matter
of criminal law; for the normal human case is
not that of the criminal, but of the law-abiding
person on whose collar the grip of the policeman
never closes. Only, it does not follow that the
hardest cases should dictate the treatment of the
relatively soft ones.

THE SEAMY SIDE OF DETERRENCE

Let us now see what are the objections to the
Deterrent or Terrorist system.

It necessarily leaves the interests of the victim wholly out of account. It injures and de-
grades him; destroys the reputation without
which he cannot get employment; and when the
punishment is imprisonment under our system,
atrophies his powers of fending for himself in
the world. Now this would not materially hurt
anyone but himself if, when he had been duly
made an example of, he were killed like a vivi-
sected dog. But he is not killed. He is, at the
expiration of his sentence, flung out of the prison
into the streets to earn his living in a labor

market where nobody will employ an ex-prisoner, betraying himself at every turn by his ignorance of the common news of the months or years he has passed without newspapers, lamed in speech, and terrified at the unaccustomed task of providing food and lodging for himself. There is only one lucrative occupation available for him; and that is crime. He has no compunction as to Society: why should he have any? Society having for its own selfish protection done its worst to him, he has no feeling about it except a desire to get a bit of his own back. He seeks the only company in which he is welcome: the society of criminals; and sooner or later, according to his luck, he finds himself in prison again. The figures of recidivism shew that the exceptions to this routine are so few as to be negligible for the purposes of our argument. The criminal, far from being deterred from crime, is forced into it; and the citizen whom his punishment was meant to protect suffers from his depredations.

It is, in fact, admitted that the deterrent system does not deter the convicted criminal. Its real efficacy is sought in its deterrent effect on the free citizens who would commit crimes but for their fear of punishment. The Terrorist can point to the wide range of evil-doing which, not being punished by law, is rampant among us; for though a man can get himself hanged for a momentary lapse of self-control under intolerable provocation by a nagging woman, or into prison for putting the precepts of Christ above the orders of a Competent Military Authority, he can be a quite infernal scoundrel without breaking any penal law. If it be true, as it certainly is, that it is conscience and not the fear of punishment that makes civilized life possible, and that Dr. Johnson's

How small, of all that human hearts endure,
That part that laws or kings can cause or cure!

is as applicable to crime as to human activity in general, it is none the less true that commercial civilization presents an appalling spectacle of pillage and parasitism, of corruption in the press and in the pulpit, of lying advertisements which make people buy rank poisons in the belief that they are health restorers, of traps to catch the provision made for the widow and the fatherless and divert it to the pockets of company promoting rogues, of villainous oppression of the poor and cruelty to the defenceless; and it is arguable that most of this could, like burglary and forgery, be kept within bearable bounds if its perpetrators were dealt with as burglars and forgers are dealt with today. It is, let us not forget, equally arguable that if we can afford to leave so much villainy unpunished we can afford to leave all villainy unpunished. Unfortunately, we cannot afford it: our toleration is threatening our civilization. The prosperity that consists in the wicked

flourishing like a green bay tree, and the humble
and contrite hearts being thoroughly despised, is
a commercial delusion. Facts must be looked in
the face, rascals told what they are, and all men
called on to justify their ways to God and Man
up to the point at which the full discharge of
their social duties leaves them free to exercise
their individual fancies. Restraint from evil-
doing is within the rights as well as within the
powers of organized society over its members;
and it cannot be denied that the exercise of these
powers, as far as it could be made inevitable,
would incidentally deter from crime a certain
number of people with only marginal consciences
or none at all, and that an extension of the penal
code would create fresh social conscience by en-
larging the list of things which law-abiding people make it a point of honor not to do, besides
calling the attention of the community to grave
matters in which they have hitherto erred through
thoughtlessness.

But there is all the difference in the world
between deterrence as an incident of the operation of criminal law, and deterrence as its sole
object and justification. In a purely deterrent
system, for instance, it matters not a jot who is
punished provided somebody is punished and the
public persuaded that he is guilty. The effect of
hanging or imprisoning the wrong man is as de-

terrent as hanging or imprisoning the right one. This is the fundamental explanation of the extreme and apparently fiendish reluctance of the Home Office to release a prisoner when, as in the Beck case, the evidence on which he was convicted has become discredited to a point at which no jury would maintain its verdict of guilty. The reluctance is not to confess that an innocent man is being punished, but to proclaim that a guilty man has escaped. For if escape is possible deterrence shrinks almost to nothing. There is no better established rule of criminology than that it is not the severity of punishment that deters, but its certainty. And the flaw in the case of Terrorism is that it is impossible to obtain enough certainty to deter. The police are compelled to confess every year, when they publish their statistics, that against the list of crimes reported to them they can set only a percentage of detections and convictions. And the list of reported crimes can form only a percentage, how large or small it is impossible to say, but probably small, of the crimes actually committed; for it is the greatest mistake to suppose that everyone who is robbed runs to the police: on the contrary, only foolish and ignorant or very angry people do so without very serious consideration and great reluctance. In most cases it costs nothing to let the thief off, and a good deal to prosecute him. The burglar in Heartbreak House, who makes his living by breaking into people's houses, and then black-mailing them by threatening to give himself up to the police and put them to the expense and discomfort of attending his trial and giving evidence after enduring all the worry of the police enquiries, is not a joke; he is a comic dramatization of a process that is going on every day. As to the black sheep of respectable families who blackmail them by offering them the alternative of making good their thefts and frauds, even to the extent of honoring their forged cheques, or having the family name disgraced, ask any experienced family solicitor.

Besides the chances of not being prosecuted, there are the chances of acquittal; but I doubt whether they count for much except with very attractive women. Still, it is worth mentioning that juries will snatch at the flimsiest pretexts for refusing to send people who engage their sympathy to the gallows or to penal servitude, even on evidence of murder or theft which would make short work of a repulsive person.

SOME PERSONAL EXPERIENCES

Take my own experience as probably common enough. Fifty years ago a friend of mine, hearing that a legacy had been left him, lent himself the expected sum out of his employers' cash: concealed the defalcation by falsifying his accounts; and was detected before he could repay. His employers angrily resented the fraud, and had certainly no desire to spare him. But a public exposure of the affair would have involved shock to their clients' sense of security, loss of time and consequently of money, an end to all hope of his ever making good the loss, and the unpleasantness of attendance in court at the trial. All this put any recourse to the police out of the question; and my friend obtained another post after a very brief interval during which he supported himself as a church organist. This, by the way, was a quite desirable conclusion, as he was for all ordinary practical purposes a sufficiently honest man. It would have been pure mischief to make him a criminal; but that is not the present point. He serves here as an illustration of the fact that our criminal law, far from inviting prosecution, attaches serious losses and inconveniences to it.

It may be said that whatever the losses and inconveniences may be, it is a public duty to prosecute. But is it? Is it not a Christian duty not to prosecute? A man stole £500 from me by a trick. He speculated in my character with subtlety and success; and yet he ran risks of detection which no quite sensible man would have ventured on. It was assumed that I would resort to the police. I asked why. The answer was that he should be punished to deter others from similar crimes. I naturally said, "You have been punishing people cruelly ·for more than a century for this kind of fraud; and the result is that I am robbed of £500. Evidently your deterrence does not deter. What it does do is to torment the swindler for years, and then throw him back upon society, a worse man in every respect, with no other employment open to him except that of fresh swindling. Besides, your elaborate arrangements to deter me from prosecuting are convincing and effective. I could earn £500 by useful work in the time it would take to prosecute this man vindictively and worse than uselessly. So I wish him joy of his booty, and invite him to swindle me again if he can." Now this was not sentimentality. I am not a bit fonder of being swindled than other people; and if society would treat swindlers properly I should denounce them without the slightest remorse, and not grudge a reasonable expenditure of time and energy in the business. But to throw good money after bad in setting to work a wicked and mischievous routine of evil would be to stamp myself as a worse man than the swindler, who earned the money more energetically, and appropriated it no more unjustly, if less legally, than I earn and appropriate my dividends.

I must however warn our thieves that I can promise them no immunity from police pursuit if

Judicial Vengeance as an Alternative to Lynch Law . . .

they rob me. Some time after the operation just recorded, an uninvited guest came to a luncheon party in my house. He (or she) got away with an overcoat and a pocketful of my wife's best table silver. But instead of selecting my overcoat, he took the best overcoat, which was that of one of my guests. My guest was insured against theft; the insurance company had to buy him a new overcoat; and the matter thus passed out of my hands into those of the police. But the result, as far as the thief was concerned, was the same. He was not captured; and he had the social satisfaction of providing employment for others in converting into a strongly fortified obstacle the flimsy gate through which he had effected an entrance, thereby giving my flat the appearance of a private madhouse.

On another occasion a drunken woman obtained admission by presenting an authentic letter from a soft-hearted member of the House of Lords. I had no guests at the moment; and as she, too, wanted an overcoat, she took mine, and actually interviewed me with it most perfunctorily concealed under her jacket. When I called her attention to it she handed it back to me effusively; begged me to shake hands with her; and went her way.

Now these things occur by the dozen every day, in spite of the severity with which they are punished when the thief is dealt with by the police. I daresay all my readers, if not too young to have completed a representative experience, could add two or three similar stories. What do they go to prove? Just that detection is so uncertain that its consequences have no really effective deterrence for the potential offender, whilst the unpleasant and expensive consequences of prosecution, being absolutely certain, have a very strong deterrent effect indeed on the prosecutor. In short, all the hideous cruelty practised by us for the sake of deterrence is wasted: we are damning our souls at great expense and trouble for nothing.

JUDICIAL VENGEANCE

Thus we see that of the three official objects of our prison system: vengeance, deterrence, and reformation of the criminal, only one is achieved; and that is the one which is nakedly abominable. But there is a plea for it which must be taken into account, and which brings us to the root of the matter in our own characters. It is said, and it is in a certain degree true, that if the Government does not lawfully organize and regulate popular vengeance, the populace will rise up and execute this vengeance lawlessly for itself. The standard defence of the Inquisition is that without it no heretic's life would have been safe. In

Texas today the people are not satisfied with the prospect of knowing that a murderer or ravisher will be electrocuted inside a gaol if a jury can resist the defence put up by his lawyer. They tear him from the hands of the sheriff; pour lamp oil over him; and burn him alive. Now the burning of human beings is not only an expression of outraged public morality; it is also a sport for which a taste can be acquired much more easily and rapidly than a taste for coursing hares, just as a taste for drink can be acquired from brandy and cocktails more easily and rapidly than from beer or sauterne. Lynching mobs begin with negro ravishers and murderers; but they presently go on to any sort of delinquent, provided he is black. Later on, as a white man will burn as amusingly as a black one, and a white woman react to tarring and feathering as thrillingly as a negress, the color line is effaced by what professes to be a rising wave of virtuous indignation, but is in fact an epidemic of Sadism. The defenders of our penal systems take advantage of it to assure us that if they did not torment and ruin a boy guilty of sleeping in the open air, an indignant public would rise and tear that boy limb from limb.

Now the reply to such a plea, from the point of view of civilized law, cannot be too sweeping. The government which cannot restrain a mob from taking the law into its own hands is no government at all. If Landru could go to the guillotine unmolested in France, and his British prototype who drowned all his wives in their baths could be peaceably hanged in England, Texas can protect its criminals by simply bringing its civilization up to the French and British level. But indeed the besetting sin of the mob is a morbid hero worship of great criminals rather than a ferocious abhorrence of them. In any case nobody will have the effrontery to pretend that the number of criminals who excite popular feeling enough to provoke lynching is more than a negligible percentage of the whole. The theory that the problem of crime is only one of organizing, regulating, and executing the vengeance of the mob will not bear plain statement, much less discussion. It is only the retributive theory over again in its most impudent form.

Having now disposed of all the official theories as the trash they are, let us return to the facts, and deal with the hard ones first. Everyone who has any extensive experience of domesticated animals, human or other, knows that there are negatively bad specimens who have no consciences, and positively bad ones who are incurably ferocious. The negative ones are often very agreeable and even charming companions; but they beg, borrow, steal, defraud, and seduce almost by reflex action: they cannot resist the most trifling temptation. They are indulged and spared to the extreme limit of endurance; but in the end they have to be deprived of their liberty in some way. The positive ones enjoy no such tolerance. Unless they are physically restrained they break people's bones, knock out their eyes, rupture their organs, or kill them.

Then there are the cruel people, not necessarily unable to control their tempers, nor fraudulent, nor in any other way disqualified for ordinary social activity or liberty, possibly even with conspicuous virtues. But, by a horrible involution, they lust after the spectacle of suffering, mental and physical, as normal men lust after love. Torture is to them a pleasure except when it is inflicted on themselves. In scores of ways, from the habitual utterance of wounding speeches, and the contriving of sly injuries and humiliations for which they cannot be brought to book legally, to thrashing their wives and children or, as bachelors, paying prostitutes of the hardier sort to submit to floggings, they seek the satisfaction of their desire wherever and however they can.

Now in the present state of our knowledge it is folly to talk of reforming these people. By this I do not mean that even now they are all quite incurable. The cases of no conscience are sometimes, like Parsifal's when he shot the swan, cases of unawakened conscience. Violent and quarrelsome people are often only energetic people who are underworked: I have known a man cured of wife-beating by setting him to beat the drum in a village band; and the quarrels that make country life so very unarcadian are picked mostly because the quarrelers have not enough friction in their lives to keep them goodhumored.

Psycho-analysis, too, which is not all quackery and pornography, might conceivably cure a case of Sadism as it might cure any of the phobias. And psycho-analysis is a mere fancy compared to the knowledge we now pretend to concerning the function of our glands and their effect on our character and conduct. In the nineteenth century this knowledge was pursued barbarously by crude vivisectors whose notion of finding out what a gland was for was to cut it violently out and see what would happen to the victim, meanwhile trying to bribe the public to tolerate such horrors by promising to make old debauchees young again. This was rightly felt to be a villainous business; besides, who could suppose that the men who did these things would hesitate to lie about the results when there was plenty of money to be made by representing them as cures for dreaded diseases? But today we are not asked to infer that because something has happened to a violently mutilated dog it must happen also to an unmutilated human being. We can now make authentic pictures of internal organs by means of rays to which flesh is transparent. This makes it possible to take a criminal and say authoritatively that he is a case, not of original sin, but of an inefficient, or excessively efficient, thyroid gland, or pituitary gland, or adrenal gland, as the case may be. This of course does not help the police in dealing with a criminal; they must apprehend and bring him to trial all the same. But if the prison doctor were able to say "Put some iodine in this man's skilly, and his character will change," then the notion of punishing instead of curing him would become ridiculous. Of course the matter is not so simple as that; and all this endocrinism, as it is called, may turn out to be only the latest addition to our already very extensive collection of pseudo-scientific mares' nests; still, we cannot ignore the fact that a considerable case is being made out by eminent physiologists for at least a conjecture that many cases which are now incurable may be disposed of in the not very remote future by inducing the patient to produce more thyroxin or pituitrin or adrenalin or what not, or even administering them to him as thyroxin is at present administered in cases of myxoedema. Yet the reports of the work of our prison medical officers suggest that hardly any of them has ever heard of these discoveries, or regards a convict as anything more interesting scientifically than a malingering rascal.

THE INCORRIGIBLE VILLAINS

It will be seen that I am prepared to go to lengths which still seem fantastic as to the possibility of changing a criminal into an honest man. And I have more faith than most prison chaplains seem to have in the possibilities of religious conversion. But I cannot add too emphatically that the people who imagine that all criminals can be reformed by setting chaplains to preach at them, by giving them pious books and tracts to read, by separating them from their companions in crime and locking them up in solitude to reflect on their sins and repent, are far worse enemies both to the criminal and to Society than those who face the fact that these are merely additional cruelties which make their victims worse, or even than those who frankly use them as a means of "giving them hell." But when this is recognized, and the bigoted reformers with their sermons, their tracts, their horrors of separation, silence, and solitude to avoid contamination, are bundled out of our prisons as nuisances, the problem remains, how are you to deal with your incorrigibles? Here you have a man who supports himself by gaining the confidence and affection of lonely women; seducing them; spending all their money; and then burning them in a stove or drowning them in a bath.

He is quite an attractive fellow, with a genuine taste for women and no taste at all for murder, which is only his way of getting rid of them when their money is spent and they are in the way of the next woman. There is no more malice or Sadism about the final operation than there is about tearing up a letter when it is done with, and throwing it into the waste paper basket. You electrocute him or hang him or chop his head off. But presently you have to deal with a man who lives in exactly the same way, but has not executive force or courage enough to commit murder. He only abandons his victims and turns up in a fresh place with a fresh name. He generally marries them, as it is easier to seduce them so.

Alongside him you have a married couple united by a passion for cruelty. They amuse themselves by tying their children to the bedstead; thrashing them with straps; and branding them with red-hot pokers. You also have to deal with a man who on the slightest irritation flings his wife under a dray, or smashes a lighted kerosene lamp into her face. He has been in prison again and again for outbursts of this kind; and always, within a week of his release, or within a few hours of it, he has done it again.

Now you cannot get rid of these nuisances and monsters by simply cataloguing them as subthyroidics and superadrenals or the like. At

present you torment them for a fixed period, at
the end of which they are set free to resume
their operations with a savage grudge against
the community which has tormented them. That
is stupid. Nothing is gained by punishing people
who cannot help themselves, and on whom deterrence is thrown away. Releasing them is like
releasing the tigers from the Zoo to find their
next meal in the nearest children's playing
ground.

THE LETHAL CHAMBER

The most obvious course is to kill them.
Some of the popular objections to this may be
considered for a moment. Death, it is said, is
irrevocable; and after all, they may turn out to
be innocent. But really you cannot handle criminals on the assumption that they may be innocent. You are not supposed to handle them at
all until you have convinced yourself by an elaborate trial that they are guilty. Besides, imprisonment is as irrevocable as hanging. Each
is a method of taking a criminal's life; and when
he prefers hanging or suicide to imprisonment
for life, as he sometimes does, he says, in effect,
that he had rather you took his life all at once,
painlessly, than minute by minute in long-drawn-
out torture. You can give a prisoner a pardon;
but you cannot give him back a moment of his

imprisonment. He may accept a reprieve willingly in the hope of a pardon or an escape or a revolution or an earthquake or what not; but as you do not mean him to evade his sentence in any way whatever, it is not for you to take such clutchings at straws into account.

Another argument against the death penalty for anything short of murder is the practical one of the policeman and the householder, who plead that if you hang burglars they will shoot to avoid capture on the ground that they may as well be hanged for a sheep as for a lamb. But this can be disposed of by pointing out, first, that even under existing circumstances the burglar occasionally shoots, and, second, that acquittals, recommendations to mercy, verdicts of manslaughter, successful pleas of insanity and so forth, already make the death penalty so uncertain that even red-handed murderers shoot no oftener than burglars—less often, in fact. This uncertainty would be actually increased if the death sentence were, as it should be, made applicable to other criminals than those convicted of wilful murder, and no longer made compulsory in any case.

Then comes the plea for the sacredness of human life. The State should not set the example of killing, or of clubbing a rioter with a policeman's baton, or of dropping bombs on a sleeping city, or of doing many things that States never-

theless have to do. But let us take the plea on
its own ground, which is, fundamentally, that life
is the most precious of all things, and its waste
the worst of crimes. We have already seen that
imprisonment does not spare the life of the criminal: it takes it and wastes it in the most cruel
way. But there are others to be considered be-
side the criminal and the citizens who fear him
so much that they cannot sleep in peace unless
he is locked up. There are the people who have
to lock him up, and fetch him his food, and watch
him. Why are their lives to be wasted? Warders, and especially wardresses, are almost as
much tied to the prison by their occupation, and
by their pensions, which they dare not forfeit
by seeking other employment, as the criminals
are. If I had to choose between a spell under
preventive detention among hardened criminals
in Camp Hill and one as warder in an ordinary
prison, I think I should vote for Camp Hill. Warders suffer in body and mind from their employment; and if it be true, as our examination seems
to prove, that they are doing no good to society,
but very active harm, their lives are wasted more
completely than those of the criminals; for most
criminals are discharged after a few weeks or
months; but the warder never escapes until he
is superannuated, by which time he is an older
gaolbird than any Lifer in the cells.

How then does the case stand with your incurable pathological case of crime? If you treat the life of the criminal as sacred, you find yourself not only taking his life but sacrificing the lives of innocent men and women to keep him locked up. There is no sort of sense or humanity in such a course. The moment we face it frankly we are driven to the conclusion that the community has a right to put a price on the right to live in it. That price must be sufficient self-control to live without wasting and destroying the lives of others, whether by direct attack like a tiger, parasitic exploitation like a leech, or having to be held in a leash with another person at the end of it. Persons lacking such self-control have been thrust out into the sage-brush to wander there until they die of thirst, a cruel and cowardly way of killing them. The dread of clean and wilful killing often leads to evasions of the commandment "Thou shalt not kill" which are far more cruel than its frank violation. It has never been possible to obey it unreservedly, either with men or with animals; and the attempts to keep the letter of it have led to burying vestal virgins and nuns alive, crushing men to death in the press-yard, handing heretics over to the secular arm, and the like, instead of killing them humanely and without any evasion of the heavy responsibility involved. It was a horrible thing to build a vestal virgin into a wall with

food and water enough for a day; but to build
her into a prison for years as we do, with just
enough loathsome food to prevent her from dy-
ing, is more than horrible: it is diabolical. If no
better alternatives to death can be found than
these, then who will not vote for death? If people are fit to live, let them live under decent human conditions. If they are not fit to live, kill
them in a decent human way. Is it any wonder
that some of us are driven to prescribe the lethal
chamber as the solution for the hard cases which
are at present made the excuse for dragging all
the other cases down to their level, and the only
solution that will create a sense of full social responsibility in modern populations?

THE SIXTH COMMANDMENT

The slaughtering of incorrigibly dangerous
persons, as distinguished from the punitive execution of murderers who have violated the commandment not to kill, cannot be established summarily by these practical considerations. In spite
of their cogency we have not only individuals
who are resolutely and uncompromisingly opposed to slaying under any provocation whatever, we have nations who have abolished the
death penalty, and regard our grim retention of

The Sixth Commandment

it as barbarous. Wider than any nation we have
the Roman Catholic Church, which insists literally on absolute obedience to the commandment,
and condemns as murder even the killing of an
unborn child to save the mother's life. In practice this obligation has been evaded so grossly—
by the Inquisition, for example, which refused to
slay the heretic, but handed him over to the
secular arm with a formal recommendation to
mercy, knowing that the secular arm would immediately burn him—that the case of the Church
might be cited to illustrate the uselessness of
barring the death penalty. But it also illustrates
the persistence and antiquity of a point of conscience which still defies the argument from expediency. That point of conscience may be called
a superstition because it is as old as the story
of Cain and Abel, and because it is difficult to
find any rational basis for it. But there is something to be said for it all the same.

Killing is a dangerously cheap way out of a
difficulty. "Stone dead hath no fellow" was a
handy formula for Cromwell's troops in dealing
with the Irish; still, that precedent is not very
reassuring. All the social problems of all the
countries can be got rid of by extirpating the in-
habitants; but to get rid of a problem is not to
solve it. Even perfectly rational solutions of our
problems must be humane as well if they are to

be accepted by good men; otherwise the logic of
the inquisitor, the dynamiter, and the vivisec-
tionist would rule the world for ever as it unfortunately does to far too great an extent already. It may also be argued that if society
were to forgo its power of slaying, and also its
practice of punishment, it would have a stronger
incentive to find out how to correct the apparently incorrigible. Although whenever it has
renounced its power to slay sane criminals it has
substituted a horribly rigorous and indeed vir-
tually lethal imprisonment, this does not apply
to homicidal lunatics, the comparatively lenient
treatment of whom could obviously be extended
to sane murderers. The Oxford Dictionary owes
several of its pages to a homicide who was detained at Broadmoor (the English Asylum for
Criminal Lunatics) during the pleasure of the
Crown. As to the cases which, when not disposed of by the lethal method, involve caging
men as tigers are caged, can they not be dealt
with by the padded room? Granted that it is
questionable whether the public conscience which
tolerates such caging is really more sensitive or
thoughtful than that which demands the lethal
solution, and that at the present time executions,
and even floggings, do not harden the authorities
and lower the standard of humanity all through
our penal system as much as continuing penalties

do, yet the reluctance to kill persists. The moment it is pointed out that if we kill incurable criminals we may as well also kill incurable troublesome invalids, people realize with a shock that the urge of horror, hatred, and vengeance is needed to nerve them—or unnerve them—to slay.. When I force humane people to face their political powers of life and death apart from punishment as I am doing now, I produce a terrified impression that I want to hang everybody. In vain I protest that I am dealing with a very small class of human monsters, and that as far as crime is concerned our indiscriminate hanging of wilful murderers and traitors slays more in one year than dispassionate lethal treatment would be likely to slay in ten. I am asked at once who is to be trusted with the appalling responsibility of deciding whether a man is to live or die, and what government could be trusted not to kill its enemies under the pretence that they are enemies of society.

The reply is obvious. Such responsibilities must be taken, whether we are fit for them or not, if civilized society is to be organized. No unofficial person denies that they are abused: the whole effect of this essay is to shew that they are horribly abused. I can say for my own part as a vehement critic and opponent of all the governments of which I have had any experience that I am the last person to forget that governments use the criminal law to suppress and exterminate their opponents whenever the opposition becomes really acute, and that the more virtuous the revolutionist and the more vicious the government, the more likely it is to kill him, and to do so under pretence of his being one of the dangerous persons for whom the lethal treatment would be reserved. It has been pointed out again and again that it is in the very nature of power to corrupt those to whom it is entrusted, and that to God alone belongs the awful prerogative of dismissing the soul from the body. Tolstoy has exhausted the persuasions of literary art in exhorting us that we resist not evil; and men have suffered abominable persecutions sooner than accept military service with its chief commandment, Thou shalt kill.

All this leaves the problem just where it was. The irresponsible humanitarian citizen may indulge his pity and sympathy to his heart's content, knowing that whenever a criminal passes to his doom there, but for the grace of God, goes he; but those who have to govern find that they must either abdicate, and that promptly, or else take on themselves as best they can many of the attributes of God. They must decide what is good and what evil; they must force men to do certain things and refrain from doing certain other things whether individual consciences approve or not; they must resist evil resolutely and continually, possibly and preferably without malice or revenge, but certainly with the effect of disarming it, preventing it, stamping it out, and creating public opinion against it. In short, they must do all sorts of things which they are manifestly not ideally fit to do, and, let us hope, do with becoming misgiving, but which must be done, all the same, well or ill, somehow and by somebody. If I were to ignore this, everyone who has had any experience of government would throw these pages aside as those of an inexperienced sentimentalist or an Impossibilist Anarchist.

Nevertheless, certain lines have to be drawn limiting the activities of governments, and allowing the individual to be a law unto himself. For instance, we are obliged (if we are wise) to tolerate sedition and blasphemy to a considerable extent because sedition and blasphemy are nothing more than the advocacy of changes in the established forms of government, morals, and religion; and without such changes there can be no social evolution. But as governments are not always wise, it is difficult enough to secure this intellectual anarchy, or as we call it, freedom of speech and conscience; and anyone who proposed to extend it to such actions as are contemplated by the advocates of lethal treatment would be dismissed as insane. No country at peace will tolerate murder, whether it is done on principle or in sin. What is more, no country at war will tolerate a refusal to murder the enemy. Thus, whether the powers of the country are being exercised for good or evil, they never remain in abeyance, and whoever proposes to set to those powers the limit of an absolute obedience to the commandment "Thou shalt not kill," must do so quite arbitrarily. He cannot give any reason that I can discover for saying that it is wickeder to break a man's neck than to cage him for life: he can only say that his instinct places an overwhelming ban on the one and not on the other; and he must depend on the existence of a similar instinct in the community for his success in having legal slaying ruled out.

THE RUTHLESSNESS OF
THE PURE HEART

In this he will have little difficulty as long as the slaying is an act of revenge and expiation, as it is at present: that is why capital punishment has been abolished in some countries, and why its abolition is agitated for in the countries which still practise it. But if these sinful ele-

ments be discarded, and the slaying is made a
matter of pure expediency, the criminal being
pitied as sincerely as a mad dog is pitied, the
most ardent present advocate of the abolition of
capital punishment may not only consent to the
slaying as he does in the case of the mad dog,
but even demand it to put an end to an unen-
durable danger and horror. Malice and fear are
narrow things, and carry with them a thousand
inhibitions and terrors and scruples. A heart
and brain purified of them gain an enormous
freedom; and this freedom is shewn not only in
the many civilized activities that are tabooed in
the savage tribe, but also in the ruthlessness with
which the civilized man destroys things that the
savage prays to and propitiates. The attempt to
reform an incurably dangerous criminal may
come to be classed with the attempt to propitiate
a sacred rattlesnake. The higher civilization
does not make still greater sacrifices to the
snake: it kills it.

I am driven to conclude, that though, if voluntary custodians can be found for dangerous
incorrigibles, as they doubtless can by attaching
compensating advantages to their employment,
it is quite possible to proceed with slaying absolutely barred, there is not enough likelihood of
this renunciation by the State of the powers of
life and death to justify me in leaving lethal

treatment out of the question. In any case it would be impossible to obtain any clear thinking on the question unless its possibilities were frankly faced and to some extent explored. I have faced them frankly and explored them as far as seems necessary; and at that I must leave it. Nothing that I have to say about the other sorts of criminals will be in the least invalidated if it should be decided that killing is to be ruled out. I think it quite likely that it may be ruled out on sentimental grounds. By the time we have reached solid ground the shock of reintroducing it (though this has been effected and even clamored for in some countries) may be too great to be faced under normal conditions. Also, as far as what we call crime is concerned, the matter is not one of the first importance. I should be surprised if, even in so large a population as ours, it would ever be thought necessary to extirpate one criminal as utterly unmanageable every year; and this means, of course, that if we decide to cage such people, the cage need not be a very large one.

I am not myself writing as an advocate one way or the other. I have to deal with European and American civilization, which, having no longer than a century ago executed people for offences now punished by a few months or even weeks of imprisonment, has advanced to a point at which less than half a dozen crimes are punishable by death: murder, piracy, rape, arson, and (in Scotland) vitriol throwing. The opponents of capital punishment usually believe, naturally enough, that the effect of abandoning the notion of punishment altogether as sinful (which it is) will sweep away the scaffold from these crimes also, and thus make an end of the death penalty. No doubt it will; but I foresee that it will reintroduce the idea of killing dangerous people simply because they are dangerous, without the least desire to punish them, and without specific reference to the actions which have called attention to their dangerousness. That extremity may be met with an absolute veto, or it may not. I cannot foresee which side I should take: a wise man does not ford a stream till he gets to it. But I am so sure that the situation will arise, that I have to deal with it here as impersonally as may be, without committing myself or anyone else one way or the other.

Now let us look at the other end of the scale, where the soft cases are. Here we are confronted with the staggering fact that many of our prisoners have not been convicted of any offence at all. They are awaiting their trial, and are too poor and friendless to find bail; whilst others have been convicted of mere breaches of by-laws of which they were ignorant, and which they could not have guessed by their sense of right and wrong; for many by-laws have no ethical character whatever. For example, a boy sells a newspaper on the premises of a railway company, and thereby infringes a by-law the object of which is to protect the commercial monopoly of the newsagents who have paid the company for the right to have a bookstall on the platform. The boy's brother jostles a passenger who is burdened with hand luggage, and says "Carry your bag, sir?" These perfectly innocent lads are sent to prison, though the warders themselves admit that a sentence of imprisonment is so ruinous to a boy's morals that they would rather see their own sons dead than in prison.

But let us take the guilty. The great majority of them have been convicted of petty frauds compared to which the common practices of the commercial world are serious crimes. Herbert Spencer's essays on the laxity of the morals of trade have called no trader successfully to repentance. It is not too much to say that any contractor in Europe or America who does not secure business by tenders and estimates and specifications for work and materials which he has not the smallest intention of doing or putting in, and who does not resort to bribery to have the work and materials he actually does do and put in passed by anybody whose duty it is to check them, is an exceptional man. The usage is so much a matter of course, and competition has made it so compulsory, that conscience is awakened only when the fraud is carried to some unusual length. I can remember two cases which illustrate what I mean very well. A builder of high commercial standing contracted to put up a public building. When the work began he found that the clerk of the works, whose business it was to check the work on behalf of the purchaser, lived opposite the building site. The contractor immediately protested that this was not part of the bargain, and that his estimate had been obtained on false pretences. The other is the case of the omnibus conductors of London when the alarum punch was invented and introduced. They immediately struck for higher wages, and got them, frankly on the ground that the punch had cut off the percentage they had been accustomed to add to their wages by peculation, and that it should be made up to them.

Both these cases prove that dishonesty does not pay when it becomes general. The contractor might just as well estimate for the work he really does and the material he actually uses; for, after all, since his object is to tempt the purchaser by keeping prices down, he has to give him the benefit of the fraud. If the purchaser finds him out and says, for example, "You estimated for galvanized pipes; and you have put in plain ones," the contractor can reply, "If I had put in galvanized pipes I should have had to charge you more." In the same way, the bus conductors might just as well have struck for an increase of wage as stolen it: the event proved they could have got it. But they thought they could secure employment more easily by asking for a low wage and making it up to their needs surreptitiously. It is one of the grievances of clerks in many businesses that they have to connive at dishonest practices as part of the regular routine of the office; but neither they nor their employers are any the richer, because business always finally settles down to the facts, and is conducted in terms not of the pretence but of the reality.

MOST PRISONERS NO WORSE THAN OURSELVES

We may take it, then, that the thief who is in prison is not necessarily more dishonest than his fellows at large, but mostly only one who, through ignorance or stupidity, steals in a way that is not customary. He snatches a loaf from the baker's counter and is promptly run into gaol. Another man snatches bread from the tables of hundreds of widows and orphans and simple credulous souls who do not know the ways of company promoters; and, as likely as not, he is run into Parliament. You may say that the remedy for this is not to spare the lesser offender but to punish the greater; but there you miss my present point, which is, that as the great majority of prisoners are not a bit more dishonest naturally than thousands of people who are not only at liberty, but highly pampered, it is no use telling me that society will fall into anarchic dissolution if these unlucky prisoners are treated with common humanity. On the contrary, when we see the outrageous extent to which the most shamelessly selfish rogues and rascals can be granted not only impunity but encouragement and magnificent remuneration, we are tempted to ask ourselves have we any right to restrain anyone at all from doing his worst to us. The first prison I ever saw had inscribed on it "Cease to Do Evil: Learn to Do Well"; but as the inscription was on the outside, the prisoners could not read it. It should have been addressed to the self-righteous free spectator in the street, and should have run "All Have Sinned, and Fallen Short of the Glory of God."

We must get out of the habit of painting human character in soot and whitewash. It is not true that men can be divided into absolutely honest persons and absolutely dishonest ones. Our honesty varies with the strain put on it; this is proved by the fact that every additional penny of income tax brings in less than the penny preceding. The purchaser of a horse or motor-car has to beware much more carefully than the purchaser of an article worth five shillings. If you take Landru at one extreme, and at the other the prisoner whose crime is sleeping out: that is to say, whose crime is no crime at all, you can place every sane human being, from the monarch to the tramp, somewhere on the scale between them. Not one of them has a blank page in the books of the Recording Angel. From the people who tell white lies about their ages, social positions, and incomes, to those who grind the faces of the poor, or marry whilst suffering from contagious disease, or buy valuable properties from inexperienced owners for a tenth of their value, or sell worthless shares for the whole of a widow's savings, or obtain vast sums on false pretences held forth by lying advertisements, to say nothing of bullying and beating in their homes, and drinking and debauching in their bachelorhood, you could at any moment find dozens of people who have never been imprisoned and never will be, and are yet worse citizens than any but the very worst of our convicts. Much of the difference between the bond and the free is a difference in circumstances only: if a man is not hungry, and his children are ailing only because they are too well fed, nobody can tell whether he

would steal a loaf if his children were crying for bread and he himself had not tasted a mouthful for twenty-four hours. Therefore, if you are in an attitude of moral superiority to our convicts: if you are one of the Serve Them Right and Give Them Hell brigade, you may justly be invited, in your own vernacular, either to Come Off It, or else Go Inside and take the measure you are meting out to others no worse than yourself.

The distinction between the people the criminal law need deal with and those it may safely leave at large is not a distinction between depravity and good nature; it is a distinction between people who cannot, as they themselves put it, go straight except in leading strings, and those who can. Incurable criminals make well-behaved soldiers and prisoners. The war of 1914-18 almost emptied our prisons of able-bodied men; and in the leading strings of military discipline these men ceased to be criminals. Some soldiers who were discharged with not only first-rate certificates of their good conduct as soldiers but with a Victoria Cross "For Valor," were no sooner cast adrift into ordinary civil life than they were presently found in the dock pleading their military services and good character as soldiers in mitigation of sentences of imprisonment for frauds and thefts of the meanest sort. When we consider how completely a soldier is enslaved by military discipline, and how abhorrent military service consequently is to civically capable people, we cannot doubt, even if there were no first-hand testimony on the subject, that many men enlist voluntarily, not because they want to lead a drunken and dissolute life (the reason given by the Iron Duke), or because they are under any of the romantic illusions on which the recruiting sergeant is supposed to practise, but because they know themselves to be unfit for full moral responsibility, and conclude that they had better have their lives ordered for them than face the effort (intolerably difficult for them) of ordering it themselves.

This effort is not made easier by our civilization. A man who treated his children as every laborer treated them as a matter of course a hundred years ago would now be imprisoned for neglecting them and keeping them away from school. The statute book is crammed with offences unknown to our grandfathers and unintelligible to uneducated men; and the list needs startling extension; for, as Mr. H. G. Wells has pointed out, its fundamental items date from the Mosaic period, when modern Capitalism, which involves a new morality, was unknown. In more obvious matters we notice how the standard of dress, manners, and lodging which qualifies a man socially for employment as a factory hand or

mechanic has risen since the days when no person
of any refinement could travel, as everybody now
travels, third-class.

REMEDIES IN THE ROUGH

We may now begin to arrange our problem
comprehensively. The people who have to be
dealt with specially by the Government because
for one reason or another they cannot deal sat-
isfactorily with themselves may be roughly divided into three sections. First, the small number of dangerous or incorrigibly mischievous human animals. With them should be associated all
hopeless defectives, from the idiot children who
lie like stranded jellyfish on asylum floors, and
have to be artificially fed, to the worst homicidal
maniacs. Second, a body of people who cannot
provide for or order their lives for themselves,
but who, under discipline and tutelage, with their
board and lodging and clothing provided for
them, as in the case of soldiers, are normally happy, well-behaved, useful citizens. (There would
be several degrees of tutelage through which
they might be promoted if they are fit and willing.) Third, all normal persons who hàve tres-
passed in some way during one of those lapses of
self-discipline which are as common as colds, and
who have been unlucky enough to fall into the

hands of the police in consequence. These last should never be imprisoned. They should be required to compensate the State for the injury done to the body politic by their misdeeds, and, when possible, to compensate the victims, as well as pay the costs of bringing them to justice. Until they have done this they cannot complain if they find themselves distrained upon; harassed by frequent compulsory appearances in court to excuse themselves; and threatened with consignment to the second class as defectives. It is quite easy to make carelessness and selfishness or petty violence and dishonesty unremunerative and disagreeable, without resorting to imprisonment. In the cases where the offender has fallen into bad habits and bad company, the stupidest course to take is to force him into the worst of all habits and the worst of all company: that is, prison habits and prison company. The proper remedies are good habits and good company. If these are not available, then the offender must be put into the second class, and kept straight under tutelage until he is fit for freedom.

The difficulty lies, it will be seen, in devising a means of dealing with the second class. The first is easy: too easy, in fact. You kill or you cage: that is all. In the third class, summoning and fining and admonishing are easy and not mischievous: you may worry a man considerably by badgering him about his conduct and dunning

him for money in a police court occasionally; but
you do not permanently disable him morally and
physically thereby. It is the offender of the second class, too good to be killed or caged, and not
good enough for normal liberty, whose treatment
bothers us.

Any proposal to place men under compulsory
tutelage immediately raises the vexed question of
what is called "the indeterminate sentence." The
British parliament has never been prevailed on
to create a possibility of a criminal being "detained preventively" for life: it has set a limit of
ten years to that condition. This is inevitable as
long as the tutelage is primarily not a tutelage
but a punishment. In England there is a law under which a drunkard, politely called an inebriate,
can voluntarily sentence himself to a term of detention for the sake of being restrained from
yielding to a temptation which he is unable to resist when left to himself. Under existing circumstances nobody is likely to do that twice, or even
once if he has any knowledge of how the unfortunate inebriates are treated. The only system
of detention available is the prison system; and
the only sort of prisoner the officials have any
practice in dealing with is the criminal. Every
detained person is therefore put through the dis-
mal routine of punishment in the first place, deterrence in the second place, and reform in the

very remote third place. The inebriate volunteer prisoner very soon finds that he is being treated as a criminal, and tries in vain to revoke his renunciation of his liberty.

Otherwise, say the authorities very truly, they would be overwhelmed with volunteers. This reminds us of the Westminster Abbey verger who charged a French gentleman with brawling in church. The magistrate, inquiring what, exactly, the foreigner had done, was told that he had knelt in prayer. "But," said the magistrate, "is not that what a church is for?" The verger was scandalized. "If we allowed that," he said, "we should have people praying all over the place." The Prison Commissioners know that if prisons were made reasonably happy places, and thrown open to volunteers like the army, they might speedily be overcrowded. And this, with its implied threat of an enormous increase of taxation, seems a conclusive objection.

THE ECONOMY ASPECT

But if its effect would be to convert a large mass of more or less dishonest, unproductive or half productive, unsatisfactory, feckless, nervous, anxious, wretched people into good citizens, it is absurd to object to it as costly. It would be unbearably costly, of course, if the life and labor of its subjects were as stupidly wasted as they are in our prisons; but any scheme into which the conditions of our present system are read will stand condemned at once. Whether the labor of the subject be organized by the State, as in Government dockyards, post offices, municipal industries and services and so forth, or by private employers obtaining labor service from the authorities, organized and used productively it must be; and anyone who maintains that such organization and production costs the nation more than wasting the labor power of able-bodied men and women either by imprisonment or by throwing criminals on the streets to prey on society and on themselves, is maintaining a monstrous capitalistic paradox. Obviously it will not cost the nation anything at all: it will enrich it and protect it. The real commercial objection to it is that it would reduce the supply of sweatable labor available for unscrupulous private employers. But so much the better if it does. Sweating may make profits for private persons here and there; but their neighbors have to pay through the nose for these profits in poor rates, police rates, public health rates (mostly disease rates), and all the rest of the gigantic expenditure, all pure waste and mischief, which falls on the ratepayer and taxpayer in his constant struggle with the fruits of the poverty which he is nevertheless invited to maintain for the sake of making two or three of his neighbors unwholesomely and unjustly rich.

It is not altogether desirable that State tutelage should be available without limit for all who may volunteer for it. We can imagine a magistrate's court as a place in which men clamoring to be literally "taken in charge" are opposed by Crown lawyers and court officials determined to prove, if possible, that these importunate volunteers are quite well able to take care of themselves if they choose. Evidence of defective character would be sternly demanded; and if these were manufactured (as in the not uncommon case of a poor woman charging her son with theft to get him taken off her hands and sent to a reformatory) the offender would be ruthlessly consigned to my third division, consisting of offenders who are not to be taken in charge at all, but simply harried and bothered and attached and sold up until they pay the damages of their offences.

But as a matter of experience men do not seek the avowed tutelage of conditions which imply deficiency of character. Most of them resent any sort of tutelage unless they are brought up to it and therefore do not feel it as an infringement of their individuality. The army and navy are not overcrowded, though the army has always been the refuge of the sort of imbecile called a ne'er-do-well. Indeed the great obstacle to realization of the Socialist dream of a perfectly organized and highly prosperous community, without poverty or overwork or idleness, is the intense repugnance of the average man to the degree of public regulation of his life which it would involve. This repugnance is certainly not weaker in England and America than elsewhere. Both Americans and Englishmen are born Anarchists; and, as complete Anarchism is practically impossible, they seek the minimum of public interference with their personal initiative, and overshoot the mark so excessively that it is no exaggeration to say that civilization is perishing of Anarchism. If civilization is to be saved for the first time in history it will have to be a much greater extension of public regulation and organization than any community has hitherto been willing to submit to. When this extension takes place it will provide the discipline of public service for large masses of the population who now look after themselves very indifferently, and are only nominally free to control their own destinies; and in this way many people of the sort that now finds itself in prison will be kept straight automatically. But in any case there is no danger of a tutelary system being swamped by a rush of volunteers qualifying themselves for it by hurling stones through shop windows or the like.

All this does not mean that we must have indeterminate sentences of tutelage. The mischief of the present system is not that the criminal under preventive detention must be released at the end of ten years, but that if he relapses he is sent to penal servitude instead of being simply and sensibly returned to Camp Hill. What it does mean is that if the tutelage be made humane and profitable, the criminal, far from demanding his discharge, will rather threaten the authorities with a repetition of his crime if they turn him out of doors. The change that is needed is to add to the present power of the detaining authorities to release the prisoner at any time if they consider him fit for self-responsibility, the power of the prisoner to reman if he finds himself more comfortable and safe under tutelage, as voluntary soldiers feel themselves more comfortable in the army, or enclosed nuns in a convent, than cast on the world on his own resources.

So much for the difficulty of the indeterminate sentence, which is quite manageable. Its discussion has led us to the discovery that in spite of the unchristian spirit of our criminal law, and the cruelty of its administration, the mere logic of facts is driving us to humane solutions. Already in England no judge or magistrate is obliged to pass any sentence whatever for a first offence except when dealing with a few extraordinary crimes which have affected our imagination so strongly that we feel bound to mark our abhorrence of them by special rigor not only to those convicted of them, but to those accused of them: for example, persons accused of high treason were formerly not allowed the help of counsel in defending themselves. And when the account of the English system of preventive detention at Camp Hill is studied in connection with the remarkable series of experiments now being made in America, it will be seen that nothing stands between us and humanity and decency but our cruelty, vindictiveness, terror, and thoughtless indifference.

CRIME IS A DISEASE

It must not be imagined that any system will reach every anti-social deed that is committed. I have already shown that most crime goes undetected, unreported, and even unforbidden; and I have suggested that if our system of dealing with crime were one with which any humane and thoughtful person could conscientiously co-operate, if we compensated injured persons for bringing criminals to justice instead of, as at present, making the process expensive and extremely disagreeable and even terrifying to them, and if we revised our penal laws by striking out of their list of criminal acts a few which ought not to be there and adding a good many which ought to be

there, we might have a good many more delin-
quents to deal with than at present unless we
concurrently improved the education and condition of the masses sufficiently to do away with
the large part of law-breaking which is merely
one of the symptoms of poverty, and would disappear with it. But in any case we should dili-
gently read Samuel Butler's Erewhon, and ac-
custom ourselves to regard crime as pathological,
and the criminal as an invalid, curable or incurable. There is, in fact, hardly an argument that
can be advanced for the stern suppression of
crime by penal methods that does not apply
equally to the suppression of disease; and we
have already an elaborate sanitary code under
which persons neglecting certain precautions
against disease are not only prosecuted but in
some instances (sometimes quite mistaken ones,
as the history of vaccination has proved) perse-
cuted very cruelly. We actually force parents to
subject their children to surgical operations,
some of which are both dangerous and highly
questionable. But we have so far stopped short
of making it a punishable offence to be attacked
by smallpox or typhus fever, though no legal assumption is more certain than that both diseases
can be extinguished by sanitation more completely than crime by education. Yet there would be
no greater injustice in such punishment than
there is in the imprisonment of any thief; and the

sanctimonious speech in which the judge in Erewhon, sentencing a man for phthisis, recapitulated the career of crime which began with an accident in childhood, and ended with pulmonary tuberculosis, was not a whit more ridiculous than the similar speeches made at every session by our own judges. Why a man who is punished for having an inefficient conscience should be privileged to have an inefficient lung is a debatable question. If one is sent to prison and the other to hospital, why make the prison so different from the hospital?

But I make the parallel here because it brings out the significance of the fact that we admit without protest that we have to put up with a good deal of illness in the world, and to treat the sufferers with special indulgence and consideration, instead of turning on them like a herd of buffaloes and goring them to death, as we do in the case of our moral invalids. We even punish people very severely for neglecting their invalids or treating them in such a way as to make them worse instead of better: that is, for doing to them exactly what we should do ourselves if instead of doing wrong in body and losing health they had gone wrong in mind and stolen a handkerchief. There are people in the world so incredibly foolish that they expect their children to be always perfectly truthful and perfectly obedient; but even these idiots do not expect their children to be perfectly well always, nor thrash them if they catch cold. In short, if crime were not punished at all, the world would not come to an end any more than it does now that disease is not punished at all. The real gist of the distinction we make is that the consequences of crime, if unpunished, are pleasant, whereas the consequences of catching a chill are its own punishment; but this will not bear examination. A bad conscience is quite as uncomfortable as a bad cold; and though there are people so hardily constituted in this respect that they can behave very selfishly without turning a hair, so are there people of such hardy physical constitution that they can abuse their bodies with impunity to an extent that would be fatal to ordinary persons. Anyhow, it is not proposed that abnormal subjects should be unrestrained.

On the other hand avoidable illnesses are just like avoidable crimes in respect of being the result of some form of indulgence, positive or negative. For all practical purposes the parallel between the physical and moral invalid holds good; only, we may have to consider the absolute sacredness of the physical invalid's life. I shall not here attempt to prejudge the result of that consideration; but it is clear that if we decide that this sacredness must be maintained at all costs, and that the idiot in Darenth, who lies there having food poured into it so that its heart may con-

Crime as a Disease . . .

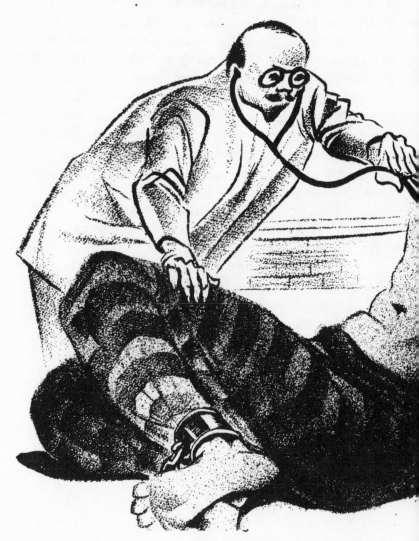

tinue to beat and its lungs to breathe automatically (for it can do nothing voluntarily), must
be preserved from death much more laboriously
than Einstein, then we must hold the criminal
equally fetish unless we are to keep the whole
subject in its present disastrous confusion.

The change in the public conscience which is
necessary before these considerations can take
effect in abolishing our villainous system of dealing with crime will never be induced by sympathy with the criminal or even disgust at the prison. The proportion of the population directly
concerned is so small that to the great majority
imprisonment is something so unlikely to occur—
indeed, so certain statistically never to occur—
that they cannot be persuaded to take any
interest in the matter. As long as the question is only one of the comfort of the prisoner, nothing will be done, because as long
as the principle of punishment is admitted,
and the Sermon on the Mount ridiculed as an
unpractical outburst of anarchism and sentimentality, the public will always be reassured by
learning from the judges (none of whom, by the
way, seems to know what really happens to a
prisoner after he leaves the dock) that our prisons are admirable institutions, and by the roman-
ces of Prison Commissioners like Du Cane and
Sir Evelyn Ruggles-Brise, who arrange prisons

as children build houses with toy bricks, and finally become so pleased with their arrangements that they describe them in terms which make us wonder that they do not commit serious crimes to qualify themselves for prolonged residence in their pet paradises. I must therefore attack the punitive position at another angle by dealing with its psychological effect on the criminal.

No ordinary criminal will agree with me for a moment that punishment is a mistake and a sin. His opinions on that point are precisely those of the policeman who arrests him; and if I were to preach this gospel of mine to the convicts in a prison I should be dismissed as a hopeless crank far more summarily than if I were to interview the Chief Commissioner at Scotland Yard about it.

Punishment is not a simple idea: it is a very complex one. It is not merely some injury that an innocent person inflicts on a guilty one, and that the guilty one evades by every means in his power. It is also a balancing of accounts with the soul. People who feel guilty are apt to inflict it on themselves if nobody will take the job off their hands. Confessions, though less common than they would be if the penalties were not so soul-destroying, are received without surprise. From the criminals' point of view punishment is expiation; and their bitterest complaints of injustice refer, not to their sentences, but to the dishonesty with which society, having exacted the price of the crime, still treats the criminal as a defaulter. Even so sophisticated a man of the world as Oscar Wilde claimed that by his two years' imprisonment he had settled accounts with the world and was entitled to begin again with a clean slate. But the world persisted in ostracizing him as if it had not punished him at all.

This was inevitable; but it was dishonest. If we are absurd enough to engage in a retributive trade in crime, we should at least trade fairly and give clean receipts when we are paid. If we did, we should soon find that the trade is impracticable and ridiculous; for neither party can deliver the goods. No discharge that the authorities can give can procure the ex-prisoner an eligible situation; and no atonement that a thief or murderer can make in suffering can make him any the less a thief or murderer. And nobody shirks this demonstration as much as the thief himself. Human self-respect wants so desperately to have its sins washed away, however purgatorially, that we are willing to go through the most fantastic ceremonies, conjurations, and ordeals to have our scarlet souls made whiter than snow. We naturally prefer to lay our sins on scapegoats or on the Cross, if our neighbors will let us off so easily; but when they will not, then we will cleanse ourselves by suffering a penalty sooner than be worried by our consciences. This is the real foundation of the criminal law in human superstition. This is why, when we refuse to employ a discharged prisoner, he invariably pleads that what he did is paid for, and that we have no right to bring it against him after he has suffered the appointed penalty.

As we cannot admit the plea, we should consider whether we should exact the penalty. I am not arguing that the plea should be admitted: I am arguing that the bargain should never have been made. I am more merciless than the criminal law, because I would destroy the evildoer's delusion that there can be any forgiveness of sin. What is done cannot be undone; and the man who steals must remain a thief until he becomes another man, no matter what reparation or expiation he may make or suffer. A punishment system means a pardon system: the two go together inseparably. Once admit that if I do something equally wicked to you we are quits when you do something equally wicked to me and you are bound to admit also that the two blacks make a white. Our criminal system is an organized attempt to produce white by two blacks. Common sense should doggedly refuse to believe that evil can be abolished by duplicating it. But common sense is not so logical; and thus we get the present grotesque spectacle of a judge committing thousands of horrible crimes in order that thousands of criminals may feel that they have balanced their moral accounts

It is a game at which there is plenty of cheating. The prisoner pleads Not Guilty, and tries his best to get off, or to have as light a sentence as possible. The commercial brigand, fining himself for his plunderings by subscribing to charities, never subscribes as much as he stole. But through all the folly and absurdity of the business, and the dense mental confusion caused by the fact that it is never frankly faced and clearly stated, there shines the fact that conscience is part of the equipment of the normal man, and that it never fails in its work. It is retributive because it makes him uncomfortable; it is deterrent because detection and retribution are absolutely certain; and it is reformative because reformation is the only way of escape. That is to say, it does to perfection by divine methods what the Prison Commissioners are trying to do by diabolical methods without hope or even possibility of success.

The effect of revenge, or retribution from without, is to destroy the conscience of the aggressor instantly. If I stand on the corn of a man in the street, and he winces or cries out, I am all remorse, and overwhelm him with heartfelt apologies. But if he sets about me with his fists, the first blow he lands changes my mind

[94]

The Criminal feels that he is working off his crime . . .

completely; and I bend all my energies on doing intentionally to his eyes and nose and jaw what I did unintentionally to his toes. Vengeance is mine, saith the Lord; and that means that it is not the Lord Chief Justice's. A violent punishing, such as a flogging, carries no sense of expiation with it: whilst its effect lasts, which is fortunately not very long, its victim is in a savage fury in which he would burn down the gaol and roast the warders and the governor and the justices alive in it with intense satisfaction if he could.

Imprisonment, on the other hand, gives the conscience a false satisfaction. The criminal feels that he is working off his crime, though he is doing it involuntarily, and would escape at any moment if he could. He preserves his sense of solvency without ceasing to be a thief, as a gambler preserves it by paying his losses without ceasing to be a gambler.

THE SENTIMENTALITY OF REVENGE

There is a mysterious psychological limit to punishment. We somehow dare not kill a hopelessly diseased or dangerous man by way of punishment for any offence short of murder, though we chloroform a hopelessly diseased or dangerous dog by way of kindness without the least mis-

giving. Until we have purged our souls of malice, which is pure sentiment, we cannot get rid of
sentimentality; and the sentimentality which
makes us abominably cruel in one direction
makes us foolishly and superstitiously afraid to
act sternly in others. Homicidal lunatics say in
their asylums "They cannot hang **us**." I could
give here, but refrain for obvious reasons, simple
instructions by carrying out which any person
can commit a murder with the certainty, if detected, of being sent to an asylum instead of to
the gallows. They ought to have just the contrary
effect; for the case of the homicidal lunatic is the
clearest case for judicial killing that exists. It is
the killing of the sane murderer that requires
consideration: it should never be a matter of
course, because there are murders which raise no
convincing presumption that those who commit
them are exceptionally likely to commit another.
But about a chronically homicidal lunatic there
should be no hesitation whatever as long as
we practise judicial killing at all; and there
would not be if we simply considered without malice the question of his fitness to live
in society. We spare him because the gallows is a
punishment, and we feel that we have no right to
punish a lunatic. When we realize that we have
no right to punish anybody, the problem of dis-
posing of impossible people will put itself on its
proper footing. We shall drop our moral airs

but unless we rule killing out absolutely, persons who give more trouble than they are worth will run the risk of being apologetically, sympathetically, painlessly but effectually returned to the dust from which they sprung.

This would at least create a sense of moral responsibility in our citizens. We are all too apt to take our lives as a matter of course. In a civilized community life is not a matter of course: it can be maintained only on complicated artifical conditions; and whoever enlarges his life by violating these conditions enlarges it at the expense of the lives of others. The extent to which we tolerate such vital embezzlement at present is quite outrageous: we have whole classes of persons who waste, squander, and luxuriate in the hard-earned income of the nation without even a pretence of social service or contribution of any kind; and instead of sternly calling on them to justify their existence or go to the scrap heap, we encourage and honor them, and indeed conduct the whole business of the country as if its object were to produce and pamper them. How can a prison chaplain appeal with any effect to the conscience of a professional criminal who knows quite well that his illegal and impecunious modes of preying on society are no worse morally, and enormously less mischievous materially, than the self-legalized plutocratic modes practised by the chaplain's most honored friends with the chaplain's full approval? The moment we cease asking whether men are good or bad, and ascertain simply whether they are pulling their weight in the social boat, our persistent evildoers may have a very unpleasant surprise. Far from having an easy time under a Government of soft-hearted and soft-headed sentimentalists, cooing that "to understand everything is to pardon everything," they may find themselves disciplined to an extent at present undreamed of by the average man-about-town.

And here it will occur to some of my readers that a book about imprisonment should be also a book about freedom. Rousseau said that Man is born free. Rousseau was wrong. No government of a civilized State can possibly regard its citizens as born free. On the contrary, it must regard them as born in debt and as necessarily incurring fresh debt every day they live; and its most pressing duty is to hold them to that debt and see that they pay it. Not until it is paid can any freedom begin for the individual. When he cannot walk a hundred yards without using such a very expensive manufactured article as a street, care must be taken that he produces his share of its cost. When he has paid scot and lot his leisure begins, and with it his liberty. He can then say boldly, "Having given unto Caesar the things that are Caesar's I shall now, under no tutelage or compulsion except that of my conscience, give to God the things that are God's." That is the only possible basis for civil liberty; and we are unable to attain it because our governments corruptly shirk the duties of Caesar; usurp the attributes of God; and make an unholy mess of which this horrible prison system of ours is only one symptom.

We must, however, be on our guard against ascribing all the villainy of that system to our cruelty and selfish terrors. I have pointed out how the operation of the criminal law is made very uncertain, and therefore loses the deterrence it aims at, by the reluctance of sympathetic people to hand over offenders to the police. Vindictive and frivolous as we are, we are not downright fiends, as we should be if our modern prison system had been deliberately invented and constructed by us all in one piece. It has grown upon us, and grown evilly, having evil roots; but its worst developments have been well meant; for the road to hell is paved with good intentions, not with bad ones. The history of it is too long to be told here in detail; but a word or two of it is needed to save the reader from closing the volume in despair of human nature.

Imprisonment was not originally a punishment any more than chaining up a dog, cruel as that practice is, is a punishment. It was simply a method of detention. The officer responsible for the custody of an offender had to lock or chain him up somewhere to prevent him from running away, and to be able to lay his hand on him on the day of trial or execution. This was regarded as the officer's own affair: the law looked to him for the delivery of the offender, and did not concern itself as to how it was effected. This seems strange nowadays; but I can remember a case of a lunatic on a battleship, who had one man told off to act as his keeper. The lunatic was violent and troublesome, and gave his keeper plenty of severe exercise; but the rest of the crew looked on with the keenest enjoyment of the spectacle, and gave the lunatic the strictest fair play by letting his keeper fight it out with him unaided. And that is what the law did mostly in England until well into the nineteenth century. To this day there is no prison in some of the Virgin Islands. The prisoner is tied by the leg to a tree and plays cards with the constable who guards him.

The result was that the provision of lock-ups became a private commercial speculation, undertaken and conducted for the sake of what could be made out of it by the speculator. There was no need for these places to be lock-ups; the accused could be chained up or gyved or manacled if no safe prison was available; and when lock-ups came to be provided as a matter of business, the practice of chaining was continued as a matter of tradition, and formed a very simple method of extorting money from prisoners by torture. No food was provided by the State: what the prisoner ate was charged against him as if he were in a hotel; and it often happened that when he was aquitted he was taken back to prison as security for his bill and kept there until he had paid it.

Under these circumstances the prison was only a building into which all classes and sorts of detained persons were thrown indiscriminately. The rich could buy a private room, like Mr. Pickwick in the Fleet; but the general herd of poor criminals, old and young, innocent and hardened, virgin and prostitute, mad and sane, clean and verminous, diseased and whole, pigged together in indescribable promiscuity. I repeat: nobody invented this. Nobody intended it. Nobody defended it except the people who made money by it. Nobody else except the prisoners knew about it: they were as innocent as Mr. Pickwick of what went on inside the prison walls. And, as usual in England, nobody bothered about it, because people with money could avoid its grossest discomforts on the negligibly rare occasions when they fell into the hands of the officers of the law. It was by the mere accident of being picked for sheriff that John Howard learned what the inside of a gaol was like.

THE CRIME OF IMPRISONMENT

As a result of Howard's agitation prisons are now State prisons: the State accepts full responsibility for the prisoner from the moment of his arrest. So far, so good. But in the meantime imprisonment, instead of being a means of detention, has become not only a punishment, but, for the reasons given at the outset of this essay, the punishment. And official shallowness, prevailing against the poet Crabbe's depth, has made it an infernal punishment. Howard saw that the prisoners in the old gaol contaminated one another; and his remedy was to give them separate cells in which they could meditate on their crimes and repent. When prisons with separate cells were built accordingly, the prison officials soon found that it saved trouble to keep the prisoners locked up in them: and the philanthropists out-Howarded Howard in their efforts to reform criminals by silence, separation, and the wearing of masks, lest they should contaminate one another by the expression of their faces. Until 1920 the convicts in Belgian prisons wore iron masks. Our own convicts wore cloth masks for some time, and would probably be wearing them still had not our solicitude for their salvation killed and driven them mad in such numbers that we were forced to admit that thorough segregation, though no doubt correct in principle (which is just where it is fatally incorrect) does not work. Frightful things in the way of solitude, separation, and silence, not for months, but for many years at a time, were done in American prisons.

The reader will find as much as he can stand in English Prisons Under Local Government, by Sidney and Beatrice Webb, and a good deal more in English Prisons Today, edited by Stephen Hobhouse and Fenner Brockway, in which the system is described from the prison cells, not by common criminals, but by educated and thoughtful men and women who, as agitators for Votes for Women or as Conscientious Objectors to military service, have been condemned to imprisonment of late years. Our horror at their disclosures must not blind us to my immediate point, which is that our prison system is a horrible accidental growth and not a deliberate human invention, and that its worst features have been produced with the intention, not of making it worse, but of making it better. Howard is not responsible: he warned us that "absolute solitude is more than human nature can bear without the hazard of distraction and despair." Elizabeth Fry saw nothing but mischief in prison silence and prison solitude. Their followers were fools: that is all.

THE SO-CALLED CRIMINAL TYPE

Perhaps the most far-reaching service done by the Brockway-Hobhouse report is the light it throws on the alleged phenomenon of a Criminal Type. The belief in this has gone through several vicissitudes. At first a criminal was supposed to be a beetle-browed, bulldog-jawed person for whom no treatment could be too bad. This suited the prison authorities, as nothing is so troublesome to them as waves of public sympathy with criminals, founded on imaginative idealizations of them. But the authorities changed their note when a scientific account of the type was put forward by Lombroso and a body of investigators calling themselves psychiatrists. These gentlemen found that criminals had asymmetrical features and other stigmata (an effective word). They contended that the criminals were the victims of these congenital peculiarities, and could not help themselves. As the obvious conclusion was that they were not morally responsible for their actions, and therefore should not be punished for them, the prison authorities saw their occupation threatened, and denied that there was any criminal type, always excepting the beetle-brows and bulldog-jaws which the criminal was assumed to have imposed on his naturally Grecian features by a life of villainy. They were able to point out that everybody has asymmetrical features, and that the alleged stigmata of the Lombrosic criminal are as characteristic of the Church, the Stock Exchange, the Bench, and the Legislature as of Portland and Dartmoor. That settled the matter for the moment. The criminal type was off.

But nobody who has ever visited a prison has any doubt that there is a prison type, and a very marked one at that. And if he is saturated with the teachings of the Natural Selectionists, according to which changes of type are the result of the slow accumulation of minute variations, and therefore cannot be visibly produced in less than, say, a million years, he will conclude, like Lombroso, that the criminal is a natural species, and therefore incorrigible.

But twentieth century observation has lately been knocking nineteenth century science into a cocked hat by shewing that the types that were said to take a million years to produce can be produced in five. I have in my hand number seventy-four of the privately printed opuscula issued by the Society which calls itself the Set of Odd Volumes. It is entitled The Influence Which Our Surroundings Exert On Us, and is the work of Sir William Arbuthnot Lane, one of our most distinguished surgeons. In it he shows that by keeping a man at work as a deal porter, a coal trimmer, a shoemaker or what not, you can, with-

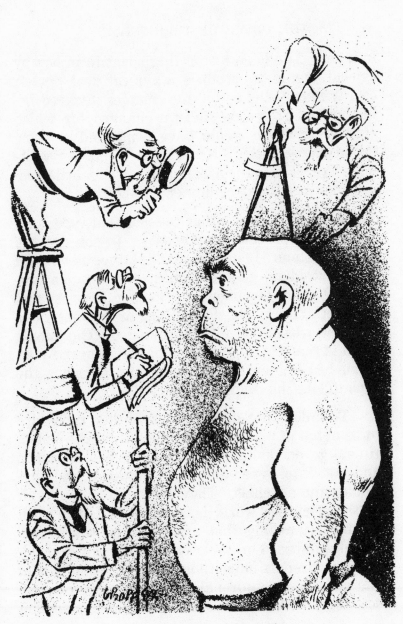

The So-Called Criminal Type

in a period no longer than that spent in prison by typical criminals, produce a typical deal porter, coal trimmer, and so on, the changes involved being visible grotesque skeletal changes for which Huxley or Owen would have demanded a whole evolutionary epoch. No Bolshevik has yet written so revolutionary a pamphlet as this little record of a recent after-dinner speech.

What it means is that the criminal type is an artificial type, manufactured in prison by the prison system. It means that the type is not one of the accidents of the system, but must be produced by imprisonment no matter how normal the victim is at the beginning, or how anxious the authorities are to keep him so. The simple truth is that the typical criminal is a normal man when he first enters a prison, and develops the type during his imprisonment.

This does not mean that no other types are to be noted in prison. By all means let the endocrinists go on dividing abnormal people, in prison and out, into hyper and sub pituitaries and thyroidics and adrenals. They need not, as the habit of the scientific world is, quarrel furiously with me for remarking that another type can be externally imposed on their pituitaries and thyroidics and adrenals impartially. The fact that a man has an excessive adrenal secretion may be a reason for trying to check it instead of punishing

him. It does not alter the fact that if you keep
one adrenal in penal servitude and another in the
House of Lords for ten years, the one will shew
the stigmata of a typical convict, and the other of
a typical peer, in addition to the stigmata of
adrenalism.

To realize the importance of this, we must
recall the discredit into which Lombroso fell
when it was pointed out that by his diagnosis
everybody was more or less a criminal. I suggest
that this was not quite so complete a **reductio ad
absurdum** as it seemed. I have already accounted
for the curious insensibility of the public to the
misery they are inflicting on their prisoners by
the fact that some of the most mischievous and
unhappy conditions of prison life are imposed on
all respectably brought-up children as a matter
of course. It is arguable that what Lombroso took
to be criminal stigmata were genuine prison stigmata, and that their prevalence among respectable people who have never been in gaol is due
to the prison conditions to which such people are
conventionally subjected for the first twenty
years of their life.

I take up another much discussed and most
readable modern book: Queen Victoria, by Lyt-
ton Strachey. It contains some shocking pages,
made bearable by the comedic power of the au-
thor, but still ghastly reading. Queen Victoria
was very carefully brought up. When she was

eighteen they came to her and told her that she was Queen of England. She asked whether she could really do what she liked; and when this was reluctantly admitted by her careful mother, Victoria considered what wonderful and hitherto impossible happiness she could confer on herself by her new powers. And she could think of nothing more delightful than an hour of separate solitary confinement. She had never been alone before, never been unwatched by people whose business it was to see that she behaved herself, and to rebuke her and punish her if she did anything they disapproved of. In short, she had been treated as a dangerous criminal, unfit to be trusted with any initiative or moral responsibility.

It would carry me too far to trace the effects of this monstrous bringing-up on the course of history. The book should be given to every prisoner who finds his solitary confinement every day from half-past four in the afternoon to next morning more than he can bear. He will find that there are worse things than solitude when the only company available is that of the warders and governor. And he will understand why the next thing the queen did was to turn her mother practically out of the house. She was, as he would put it, getting a bit of her own back. Let him then, if he is an intellectually curious prisoner, and has not been long enough in prison to have his intellect atrophied, make a list of the miseries that are common to the lot of our little Queen Victorias out of prison and our thieves and murderers in prison. · Confinement, obedience, silence at associated work, continual supervision by hostile guardians reporting every infraction of rule for punishment, regulation of every moment of one's life from outside, compulsory exercise instead of play, systematic extirpation of initiative and responsibility, uncongenial and sometimes impossible tasks, and a normal assumption that every original and undictated action will be a wrong action. This is the lot of the well-brought-up child, whether heiress to a throne or heir to a country rector, like Samuel Butler, who was beaten by his father until he acquired and retained until his death some of the stigmata of a chained dog. The British statesman Mr. Winston Churchill, a duke's grandson, tells us in his reminiscences that when he was a child of seven he was sent to an expensive school where the discipline was more ferocious than would be permitted in a Reformatory for young criminals of twice that age.

Butler, a man of exceptionally strong character which reacted violently against his training, would have been what the Prison Commissioners call a bad prisoner, and therefore does not illustrate the normal social effect of the system. Even Queen Victoria, with all her characteristic prison transitions from tutelage to tyranny, and her inability to understand or tolerate any other conditions, was too energetic, uneducated, and original, not to react vigorously against her circumstances. It is when we look at modern civilization in bulk that we are forced to admit that child training (or rather taming), as we practise it, produces moral imbecility. About a dozen millions of persons, on whose education enormous sums had been spent publicly and privately, went like sheep to the slaughter in 1914-18; and the survivors are making elaborate arrangements to go again. A glance at the newspapers which cater specially for the classes which go through the respectable routine of preparatory school, public school, and university, will shew that the ideals of those classes, their points of honor, their sense of humor, their boasts, their anticipations of future exploits, are precisely those of criminals. They always are ready (Steady, boys, steady) to fight and to conquer again and again. Ned Kelly, Charles Peace, Dick Turpin and Claude Duval, the Black Prince, Harry the Fifth, Robin Hood, Paul Jones, Clive, Nelson and Captain Kidd, Cortez and Lord Roberts, were not all on the side of the law; but their morality was the same: they all held that pugnacity, the will to conquer, and the sort of courage that makes pugnacity and the will to conquer effective, are virtues so splendid that they sanctify plunder, devastation, and murder in direct pro-

portion to the magnitude of these operations. The
relaxations of the operators are love affairs and
luxurious banquets. Now pray what else is the
romance of the thieves' kitchen and of the sur-
reptitious conversations of the prison exercise
ring and associated labor shop? The difference
is no more essential than that between whiskey
and champagne, between an ounce of shag and a
box of Havanas, between a burglary and a bom-
bardment, between a jemmy and a bayonet, between a chloroformed pad and a gas shell, between a Browning pistol bought at a pawnbrok-
er's and a service revolver. Gild the reputable end
of it as thickly as we like with the cant of courage, patriotism, national prestige, security, duty,
and all the rest of it: smudge the disreputable
end with all the vituperation that the utmost
transports of virtuous indignation can inspire:
such tricks will not induce the divine judgment,
by which all mankind must finally stand or fall,
to distinguish between the victims of these two
bragging predatory insects, the criminal and the
gentleman.

The gentleman beats the criminal hollow in
the magnitude of his operations and the number
of people employed in them. For the depredations of the criminal are negligibly small compared
to the military holocausts and ravaged areas, the
civic slums, the hospitals, the cemeteries crowded
with the prematurely dead, and the labor markets

in which men and women are exposed for sale for all purposes honorable and dishonorable. These are the products of criminal ideas imposed on the entire population. The common thief and burglar, miserably sweated by the receiver to whom he has to sell his plunder, steals a few spoons or diamonds at monstrous risk, and gets less than a tenth of their value from a rascal who runs no risk worth considering; and the poor wretch is content with the trumpery debauch his hard-earned percentage brings him. The gentleman steals a whole country, or a perpetual income for himself and his descendants, and is never satisfied until he has more conquests and more riches to boast of. What is more, the illicit thief does not defend his conduct ethically. He may cry "To hell with the parsons and with honesty and white-livered respectability!" and so forth; but he does so as a defier of God, a public enemy, a Satanic hero. The gentleman really believes that he is a creator of national prestige, a defender of the faith, a pillar of society; and with this conviction to strengthen him he is utterly unscrupulous in his misplaced pride and honor, and plays the wholesaler in evil to the criminal's petty retail enterprises.

THE ROOT OF THE EVIL

And what is at the bottom of it all? Just the belief that virtue is something to be imposed on us from without, like the tricks taught to a performing animal, by the whip. Such manufactured virtue has no ethical value whatever, as appears promptly enough when the whip is removed. All communities must live finally by their ethical values: that is, by their genuine virtues. Living virtuously is an art that can be learnt only by living in full responsibility for our own actions; and as the process is one of trial and error even when seeking the guidance of others' experience, society must, whether it likes it or not, put up with a certain burden of individual error The man who has never made a mistake will never make anything; and the man who has never done any harm will never do any good. The disastrous people are the indelicate and conceited busybodies who want to reform criminals and mould children's characters by external pressure and abortion. The cowards who refuse to accept the inevitable risks of human society, and would have everybody handcuffed if they could lest they should have their pockets picked or their heads punched, are bad enough; and the flagellomaniacs who are forever shrieking the exploded falsehood that garotting was put down by flogging,

and that all crimes, especially the sexually excit-
ing ones, can be put down by more flogging, are
worse; but such obvious cases of phobia and li-
bido soon make themselves ridiculous if they are
given a free platform. It is the busybody, the
quack, the pseudo God Almighty, the Dr. Moreau
of Mr. H. G. Wells' ghastliest romance, continually lusting to lay hands on living creatures and
by reckless violation of their souls and bodies
abort them into some monster representing their
ideal of a Good Man, or a Model Citizen, or a Per-
fect Wife and Mother: he is the irreconcilable enemy, the ubiquitous and iniquitous nuisance, and
the most difficult to get rid of because he has
imposed his moral pretensions on public opinion,
and is accepted as just the sort of philanthropist
our prisons and criminals should be left to,
whereas he (or she) is really the only sort of person who should never be admitted to any part of
a prison except the gallows on which so many less
mischievous egotists have expired. No one who
has not a profound instinctive respect for the
right of all living creatures to moral and religious
liberty: that is, to liberty of moral and religious
experiment on themselves, limited only by their
obligations not to become unduly burdensome to
others, should be let come within ten miles of a
child, a criminal, or any other person in a condition of tutelage. Indelicacy on this point is the
most conclusive of social disqualifications. When

it is ignorant and short-sighted it produces criminals. When it is worldly-wise and pompous it produces Prison Commissioners.

For the reader's mental convenience, I recapitulate the contentions presented above.

1. Modern imprisonment: that is, imprisonment practised as a punishment as well as a means of detention, is extremely cruel and mischievous, and therefore extremely wicked. The word extremely is used advisedly because the system has been pushed to a degree at which prison mortality and prison insanity forced it back to the point at which it is barely endurable, which point may therefore be regarded as the practicable extreme.

2. Although public vindictiveness and public dread are largely responsible for this wickedness, some of the most cruel features of the prison system are not understood by the public, and have not been deliberately invented and contrived for the purpose of increasing the prisoner's torment. The worst of these are (a) unsuccessful attempts at reform, (b) successful attempts to make the working of the prison cheaper for the State and easier for the officials, and (c) accidents of the evolution of the old privately owned detention prison into the new punitive State prison.

3. The prison authorities profess three ob-

jects: (a) Retribution (a euphemism for vengeance), (b) Deterrence (a euphemism for Terrorism), and (c) Reform of the prisoner. They achieve the first by simple atrocity. They fail in the second through lack of the necessary certainty of detention, prosecution, and conviction; partly because their methods are too cruel and mischievous to secure the co-operation of the public; partly because the prosecutor is put to serious inconvenience and loss of time; partly because most people desire to avoid an unquestionable family disgrace much more than to secure a very questionable justice; and partly because the proportion of avowedly undetected crimes is high enough to hold out reasonable hopes to the criminal that he will never be called to account. The third (Reform) is irreconcilable with the first (Retribution); for the figures of recidivism, and the discovery that the so-called Criminal Type is really a prison type, prove that the retributive process is one of uncompensated deterioration.

4. The cardinal vice of the system is the anti-Christian vice of vengeance, or the intentional duplication of malicious injuries partly in pure spite, partly in compliance with the expiatory superstition that two blacks make a white. The criminal accepts this, but claims that punishment absolves him if the injuries are equivalent, and still more if he has the worse of the bargain, as

he almost always has. Consequently, when abso-
lution on his release is necessarily denied him,
and he is forced back into crime by the refusal
to employ him, he feels that he is entitled to revenge this injustice by becoming an enemy of society. No beneficial reform of our treatment of
criminals is possible unless and until this superstition of expiation and this essentially sentimental vice of vengeance are unconditionally eradi-
cated.

5. Society has a right of self-defence, extend-
ing to the destruction or restraint of lawbreakers. This right is separable from the right to revenge or punish: it need have no more to do with
punishment or revenge than the caging or shoot-
ing of a man-eating tiger. It arises from the existence of (A) intolerably mischievous human beings, and (B) persons defective in the self-control needed for free life in modern society, but
well behaved and at their ease under tutelage and
discipline. Class A can be painlessly killed or
permanently restrained. The requisite tutelage
and discipline can be provided for Class B without rancor or insult. The rest can be treated not
as criminals but as civil defendants, and made to
pay for their depredations in the same manner.
At present many persons guilty of conduct much
viler than that for which poor men are sent to
prison suffer nothing worse than civil actions

The Root of the Evil

for damages when they do not (unhappily) enjoy complete impunity.

6. The principle to be kept before the minds of all citizens is that as civilized society is a very costly arrangement necessary to their subsistence and security they must justify their enjoyment of it by contributing their share to its cost, and giving no more than their share of trouble, subject to every possible provision by insurance against innocent disability. This is a condition precedent to freedom, and justifies us in removing cases of incurable noxious disability by simply putting an end to their existence.

7. An unconquerable repugnance to judicial killing having led to the abolition of capital punishment in several countries, and to its reservation for specially dangerous or abhorrent crimes in all the others, it is possible that the right to kill may be renounced by all civilized States. This repugnance may be intensified as we cease to distinguish between sin and infirmity, or, in prison language, between crime and disease, because of our fear of being led to the extirpation of the incurable invalid who is excessively troublesome as well as to that of the incurable criminal.

On the other hand, the opposite temperament, which is not squeamish about making short work of hard cases, and which is revolted by the daily sacrifice of the lives of prison officials, and of relatives and nurses, to incurable criminals and invalids, may be reinforced by the abandonment of ethical pretentiousness, vengeance, malice, and all uncharitableness in the matter, and may become less scrupulous than at present in advocating euthanasia for all incurables.

Whichever party may prevail, punishment as such is likely to disappear, and with it the earmarking of certain offences as calling for specially deterrent severities. But it does not follow that lethal treatment of extreme cases will be barred. On the contrary, it may be extended from murder to social incompatibility of all sorts. If it be absolutely barred, sufficient restraint must be effected, not as a punishment but as a necessity for public safety. But there will be no excuse for making it more unpleasant that it need be.

8. When detention and restraint are necessary, the criminal's right to contact with all the spiritual influences of his day should be respected, and its exercise encouraged and facilitated. Conversation, access to books and pictures and music, unfettered scientific philosophic, and religious activity, change of scene and occupation, the free formation of friendships and acquaintances, marriage and parentage: in short, all the normal methods of creation and recreation, must be available for criminals as for other persons, partly because deprivation of these things is se-

verely punitive, and partly because it is destructive to the victim, and produces what we call the criminal type, making a cure impossible. Any specific liberty which the criminal's specific defects lead him to abuse, will, no doubt, be taken from him; but if his life is spared his right to live must be accepted in the fullest sense, and not, as at present, merely as a right to breathe and circulate his blood. In short, a criminal should be treated, not as a man who has forfeited all normal rights and liberties by the breaking of a single law, but as one who, through some specific weakness or weaknesses, is incapable of exercising some specific liberty or liberties.

9. The main difficulty in applying this concept of individual freedom to the criminal arises from the fact that the concept itself is as yet unformed. We do not apply it to children, at home or at school, nor to employees, nor to persons of any class or age who are in the power of other persons. Like Queen Victoria, we conceive Man as being either in authority or subject to authority, each person doing only what he is expressly permitted to do, or what the example of the rest of his class encourages him to consider as tacitly permitted. The concept of the evolving free man in an evolving society, making all sorts of experiments in conduct, and therefore doing everything he likes as far as he can unless there are express prohibitions to which he is politically a consent-

ing party, is still unusual, and consequently terrifying, in spite of all the individualist pamphlets of the eighteenth and nineteenth centuries. It will be found that those who are most scandalized by the liberties I am claiming for the convict would be equally scandalized if I claimed them for their own sons, or even for themselves.

The conclusion is that imprisonment cannot be fully understood by those who do not understand freedom. But it can be understood quite well enough to have it made a much less horrible, wicked, and wasteful thing than it is at present.